You can win the Supermarket Game
—and beat the system!
Each year 80 billion cashoff
coupons and 7000 refund offers
help you do it. This book
will show you how to do it.

"The Supermarket Shopper's"
1980 GUIDE TO COUPONS
AND REFUNDS
By Martin Sloane
Author of the nationally
syndicated newspaper column
"The Supermarket Shopper"

1980 GUIDE TO COUPONS AND REFUNDS

Martin Sloane

BANTAM BOOKS
TORONTO · NEW YORK · LONDON

1980 GUIDE TO COUPONS AND REFUNDS
A Bantam Book / March 1980

All rights reserved.
Copyright © 1980 by Martin Sloane.
Designed by Gene Siegel
Cover art copyright © 1980 by Bantam Books, Inc.

ISBN 0–553–13723–9

Published simultaneously in the United States and Canada

Bantam Books are published by Bantam Books, Inc. Its trademark, consisting of the words "Bantam Books" and the portrayal of a bantam, is Registered in U.S. Patent and Trademark Office and in other countries. Marca Registrada. Bantam Books, Inc., 666 Fifth Avenue, New York, New York 10019.

PRINTED IN THE UNITED STATES OF AMERICA

0 9 8 7 6 5 4 3

Dedication

This book is dedicated to my loving wife June, daughter Carolyn and son Peter, who live with a husband who shops, a daddy who clips and saves, and a basement full of boxtops and labels.

A special dedication is made to my mother, Mrs. Rachel Sloane, who after the death of my father, brought up my sister and myself to appreciate super-smart shopping and the value of a dollar.

Last, but far from least, this book is dedicated to couponers and refunders everywhere.

Acknowledgements

I want to thank Ruth Brooks and the members of the American Coupon Club, without whose help this book could not have been written. I also want to mention the editors and staff of *The National Supermarket Shopper* who assisted me in many ways, in particular, Muriel Pfeifer, Susan Rothman, Denise Rigopoulos, Diane De Gennaro and Judith Kaplan. I am also grateful for the help of Arlene Winnick and Ron Dubey who assisted me in compiling the refund offers and the proof of purchase list.

Important Note

Please note that all coupons, refund forms and proofs of purchase shown in this book are reproduced solely for the purpose of providing readers with illustrations of the actual coupons and forms that they can find in newspapers, stores and other places. They ARE NOT actual offers and readers should not attempt to use them as such. They have been marked VOID to indicate that they will not be honored by stores or manufacturers.

1980 Guide To
COUPONS AND REFUNDS

Introduction

Inflation has changed supermarket shopping. Talk to any group of supermarket shoppers and you will hear remarks like these:

"I used to like shopping for food—but now I hate it!"

"When I walk into the supermarket I get a knot in my stomach."

"I could just cry every time I come home from the store with no money left and less food in my shopping bags."

But supermarket shopping doesn't have to be this way.

I can teach you how to save as much as $100 a month on national brand supermarket products you use every day!

I can show you how to save 50 percent and more on products made by companies like Armour, Buitoni, Campbell's, General Mills, Kraft, Pillsbury, and hundreds more just like them.

"Impossible" you say?

No, it is not only possible but easy, once you start couponing and refunding and use the system I developed for the American Coupon Club. More than 50,000

A.C.C. members in every state of the union are now using it to feed their families better for a lot less money.

My system shows you how to save money with the 7,000 refund offers that manufacturers will make this year, and the more than 80 billion cashoff coupons that they will distribute. This is the system that teaches you how to plan your supermarket shopping to take maximum advantage of all of these discounts and more.

Did you know that you can combine these discounts for savings of 70, 80, and even 90 percent? The proof is here in this guide, fully illustrated and easy to follow so that you can do it too.

Last year manufacturers gave away hundreds of millions of dollars—did you get your fair share? Did you save $300 to $400 with cashoff coupons? Did you receive $600 to $700 in the mail from manufacturers as refunds for purchasing their products? The chances are you threw out all the boxtops, labels, and other valuable proofs of purchase that would have entitled you to their big cash refunds.

What a waste! What you did was throw away handfuls of dollar bills!

But dry your tears. Couponing and refunding are easy to learn. Anyone can do it. All the information you need to get started is right here in this guide. The system that will bring you supermarket savings greater than you ever dreamed possible is fully explained.

This guide will open a new world to you. By the time you finish the last chapter you will have learned the secrets of couponing and refunding. You will be what I call a "super-smart shopper." It will have changed your whole outlook on supermarket shopping. You will look forward to going shopping. Each trip will now be an adventure, a savings safari that you will enjoy more than a television game show. And after the cashier adds up your savings, with other shoppers looking on in amazement, you'll walk out of the store with a big smile on your face and money in your pocket.

Welcome to The World of Couponing and Refunding.

1

To Make Super-smart Savings You Need a Super-smart System

Today, when most shoppers walk into the supermarket, they find inflation staring them in the face and they feel as if they don't have a friend.

But you do have friends in the supermarket. As you walk down the aisles you have thousands of friends. Every manufacturer wants to be your friend. They are even competing for your friendship.

"They don't look very friendly to me!"

But they are, and they will show you their friendship where it means the most—by saving you money.

This year manufacturers will make more than 7,000 refund offers. Just pick up any national brand box, bottle, or can, and the chances are you can get a refund on it.

"You mean that these manufacturers will give me my money back?"

Yes, some will give you all your money back, but

1

most manufacturers will send you refund checks for at least 25 to 50 percent of your purchase price.

Doesn't this make all these manufacturers look a little friendlier?

"Yes it does."

Manufacturers will also distribute more cashoff coupons this year than ever before: more than 80 billion of them!

They will spend millions of dollars designing the advertisements that contain these coupons. They will pay newspapers tens of millions of dollars to run these ads. And finally, they will reimburse supermarkets hundreds of millions of dollars for giving you the discounts that these coupons represent. Manufacturers really want you to cash in on their cashoff coupons.

These national brand manufacturers will often give you opportunities to use coupons and refunds for the same items. It is as if they are challenging you to be a super-smart shopper and come up with the double discounts that save you 50 percent and more.

These manufacturers look a lot friendlier don't they?

"They sure do, but there must be a catch somewhere."

Yes, there is a catch. All this friendship on the part of manufacturers can be overwhelming if you let it. Once you start clipping coupons you can collect hundreds, even thousands of them, enough to fill many drawers or shoeboxes. You can also find hundreds of refund forms, and this means even more pieces of paper to keep track of.

Unfortunately many novice coupon clippers get buried under a blizzard of coupons and wind up taking advantage of very few of them.

I remember when I started clipping coupons. Within a short time I had more than a hundred of them stuffed in an envelope. I took this envelope to the supermarket with me, but no matter how hard I tried, I couldn't use more than a few of them, unless I purchased things I really didn't need. There I was, standing at the checkout counter with $80 worth of groceries, with $25 worth of cashoff coupons in my envelope, and I couldn't save more than a dollar!

Frustrating? You bet!

I thought about it, and decided that if the manufacturers wanted to be so friendly with their discounts, the very least I could do was to get myself organized to take advantage of them.

It took me many months to get my coupons, refunds, and other supermarket discounts organized to the point where I was saving $20 a week, every week. It then took more than a year to put this knowledge into a system that any shopper could follow and use effectively.

When I knew that the system would work, I joined with Ruth Brooks in founding the American Coupon Club so that millions of other smart shoppers could benefit from it.

"Do I really need a system to take advantage of these discounts?"

YES! If you really want supermarket savings of as much as $100 a month, you can't do without one. Here's why:

- A system will help you to find as many of these discount opportunities as possible. The more you find, the more you have to choose from, and the greater your savings will be.
- Once you find all these discount opportunities, you need a system to help you file them away so that they can be easily found when you need them. Without a filing system, you will find yourself buried up to your neck in coupons and refund forms.
- You need a system that will help you get as many of these discounts as possible onto your shopping list.

You can clip all the coupons you like, but unless you can turn them into useful purchases, they aren't worth a pile of Tortilla Chips!

• A good system will also help you to spot double and even triple discounts on the same item!

"Can I really save as much as $100 a month with your system?"

YES! This guide gives you all the information you need to start saving as much as $100 a month this year, and even more next year.

"Prove it!"

You asked for proof. Here it is:

How would you like to buy a jar of Kraft Mayonnaise for just 19¢?

We don't mean a sample size. We are talking about the big 32-ounce jar that usually sells for around $1.59.

Here is how we bought it for 19¢:

First, we found a supermarket ad in the food section of our Wednesday newspaper. It offered the jar of mayonnaise at a sale priced special for $1.29—*a savings of 30¢.*

Second, we went to our coupon file folder No. 5, for Salad Dressings, and found a manufacturer's cash-off coupon that gave us *a savings of 10¢.*

Last, we went to the file box where we keep our refund forms, and found a refund offer that got us a Kraft Mayonnaise refund *saving us $1.*

!TRIPLE DISCOUNT!
Total Savings $1.40
Our Final Cost 19¢!

Amazing?

Yes it is, but the truly astonishing fact is that smart shoppers who have read this guide are finding triple discounts like this for products they use every day; products like Mueller's Egg Noodles, Betty Crocker Cake Mix, Franco American Spaghetti, Wish-Bone Salad Dressing, Ragu Spaghetti Sauce, Soup Starter, and even Cheerios.

You can do it too.

"How much time does it take?"

Once you get your files set up, successful couponing and refunding take less than five hours each week.

Is it worth the trouble? Almost every shopper I know says that it is. These few hours can save you $25 and give you twice as much enjoyment. Once you start couponing and refunding you will find it to be one of your most enjoyable activities.

Tip from *The Shopper:*

One of the secrets of successful couponing and refunding is to set up a regular time for your clipping, filing, and sending. If you spend a few hours doing it on Wednesday or Thursday evening, make it a regular event. Do it while watching television or listening to the stereo. Make these few hours your most important money saving habit.

"What is the American Coupon Club?"

The American Coupon Club is the national organization for couponers and refunders. We call it the A.C.C. for short. It now has more than 50,000 members in every state of the Union. Its members receive the Club's monthly magazine, *The National Supermarket Shopper,* and other membership benefits. The Club also charters local "A.C.C. Shoppers' Circle" coupon clubs.

In this guide we will also tell you about the World

of Couponing and Refunding; about the social life, the club meetings and the conventions.

But more about these things later.

Let's get back to saving big $$$$$$!

2

Refunds and Refund Forms

This year manufacturers will make more than 7,000 refund offers.

Smart shoppers who know the secrets of refunding will receive as much as $100 a month in refunds. Each day they look forward to receiving checks and free products in their mailbox. For them, refunding has put the fun back in shopping.

You can do it too! You can save big money just the way they do. In this chapter we will explain refunding and answer most of your questions.

What Is Refunding All About?

Imagine a manufacturer's salesman coming to your kitchen after a Sunday dinner. He pokes around in your garbage, finds the label from a can of green peas, and hands you 50¢. He smiles as he gives you a dollar for the brand name he has taken from the turkey wrapper.

But he isn't finished. He pokes around some more and happily rips the UPC symbol off the cookie box. He puts another 50¢ in your hand. Finally, he finds

7

the plastic lid from the empty coffee can. He carefully snips a piece of it and gives you a coupon for a free can of coffee.

It sounds like a flight of fancy but this is what refunding is all about; manufacturers will give you cash and free merchandise for using their products and sending the boxtops and labels that they require as proof of purchase.

Chances are that you have been throwing out the boxtops and labels that could have gotten you big cash refunds. With every bag of garbage you were throwing away handfuls of dollars.

But weep no more. You are about to become a refunder!

A Typical Refund Offer

Although refund offers may take many different forms, the Sunshine Super Sweet Offer is typical of the majority of them. Sunshine offered to send a $1 refund in return for three proofs of purchase. We abbreviate proofs of purchase as POP. In this case the POPs are purchase seals to be found on boxes of Sunshine Mallopuffs, Marshmallow Bars, or Sprinkles. Note that the refund form states that you can send all three seals from one variety or from a combination of the three.

SUNSHINE'S SUPER SWEET OFFER
$1 REFUND

SEND 3 PROOFS OF PURCHASE FROM MALLOPUFFS, MARSHMALLOW BARS OR SPRINKLES.

1.00 Refund
Sunshine Sweet Offer MMI
P.O. Box 940, El Paso, Texas 79977

Enclosed are 3 proof of purchase seals from Mallopuffs, Marshmallow Bars, or Sprinkles (any one or combination). Send my $1.00 refund to:

NAME:

ADDRESS:

CITY: STATE: ZIP:

VOID

Limit one refund per family or address. Offer good in Continental United States only, except where prohibited, taxed, or restricted by law. Allow four to six weeks to receive your refund. Offer expires September 30, 1979.

SPP-3015

"Why do manufacturers make refund offers?"

Manufacturers make refund offers because these offers help them to sell their products. Some refund offers are made to test new products and for market research, but the majority of the 7,000 refund offers that will be made this year will be to increase retail sales.

Here's how it works: Let's say that you have vegetable oil on your shopping list. When you get to the supermarket aisle that has all the vegetable oils, you find the brand you usually buy, but right next to it is a competing brand and you notice a big star on its label. In the star are the words "$1 Refund Offer." The oils look very similar, but your usual brand isn't offering you a dollar back. So, you take the plunge and add the bottle with the refund offer to your shopping cart. Manufacturers know that many shoppers can't resist a bargain and will be tempted by an offer like this. That is precisely why they make refund offers.

"How much can I save with refunds?"

As you will soon see from the examples we will show you, refund offers can save you an average of 25 percent to 50 percent of the retail price that you paid for an item. Some refunds save you much more!

In the case of the Sunshine offer, the cost of the three packages of cookies when the offer was current was $2.76. The $1 refund therefore represented a discount of 36 percent.

Free Product Offers

In return for your proofs of purchase (POPs) many manufacturers will offer you a free product rather than a cash refund.

The La Choy Single Can and Frozen Chow Meins refund form shown below is a good example of a free product offer. If you send La Choy the proofs of purchase from two of the products listed, they will send you a coupon that you can redeem at the store for a free product.

The above illustration shows the entire form, including space for your name, address, and zip code, the address to which you send the form and your proofs of purchase, and the requirements of the offer. Usually, because of space requirements, we will only show you the front of the form.

A shopper who takes advantage of a "Buy Two—Get One Free" offer is getting a one-third (33 1/3 percent) discount which is about average for most refund offers.

"Buy One—Get One Free" Offers

Refunding really gets exciting when you find 50 percent discounts with refunds like these. If you add additional coupon discounts and supermarket discounts the savings are tremendous—read on and you will learn all about it.

In most cases where a free product is offered, the manufacturer will send you a coupon which you can redeem at your supermarket for a free package of that product. The supermarket gets the retail price of the product from the manufacturer plus a small handling fee.

Full Purchase Price Refunds

Can you get free food by refunding?

Yes! You certainly can and here are just a few examples.

You will find even more free food opportunities when you learn how to make "Triple Plays" in chapter 9.

High Value Refund Offers

Are there really $3, $4, and $5 refunds?

Yes. Manufacturers are increasing the value of their refund offers. Just a few years ago the 35¢ refund was the most common. Today the average refund exceeds $1 and manufacturers are making many $2 and $3 refunds that ask for proofs of purchase from several different products.

The Dow Gift Certificate Offer shown below is an excellent example of a high value refund. The offer requires four proofs of purchase from various Dow products. At the time the offer was current their total retail price was $3.78. This $4 offer gives you a profit of

22¢! Since Dow distributes many cashoff coupons for these same products and they are often featured as supermarket specials, most couponers and refunders found it easy to make double and triple discounts on these products.

Unfortunately some manufacturers still make 35¢ refund offers. With the cost of postage at 15¢ it is hard to understand why they believe that a 35¢ offer would effectively motivate a purchase of their product. Most refunders now ignore any refund of less than 50¢.

A Note from *The Shopper*:

To simplify the various discount calculations we have not taken into account the cost of the stamp and envelope necessary to obtain your refund. As you will see, the total value of the discounts you will be able to obtain through couponing and refunding will make these costs of minor significance.

Gift Offers

Many manufacturers know that an attractive gift offer gives a shopper a strong incentive to purchase their product. The "Free Me!" perfume offer asked for two proofs of purchase from Nice 'n Easy haircolor in return for a bottle of Me Perfume which had a "$20 comparable retail value."

Similarly, if you buy 12 oz. worth of Nescafé, you can get a free World Mug.

Percent of Purchase Refund

Some refund offers give you a refund based on the total purchases shown on your cash register receipt! Of course there is a maximum, $3 shown in the All offer below, but this high value refund is certainly a good one.

Your total store purchases would have to be at least $30 in order to get the maximum benefit from the All offer. Also note the restrictions on alcohol, tobacco, poultry, milk, and dairy products.

Milk, Meat, and Produce Refunds

Are there refunds for milk, fresh meat, and produce?

Not really, but many packaged goods manufacturers will give you a refund if you have purchased these items along with their own products, or they will send you a coupon good on your next purchase of these items. So, refunding can put meat on your table and here are some examples:

A Very Special Refund Offer

The Sara Lee refund offer shown below also includes a donation to the Muscular Dystrophy Association. By sending for your $1 refund you also donate $1 to this very worthwhile cause. It is hoped that other manufacturers will follow the leadership of the people at Sara Lee.

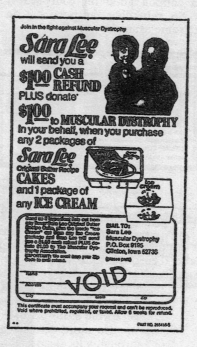

Money-Plus Offers

An increasing number of manufacturers are making offers of merchandise in return for proofs of purchase and a specified sum of money. We call them "money-plus" offers. The Palmolive Calculator offer is a good example. The offer asks for a payment of $9.99 plus one 'fl. oz.' marking from any Palmolive bottle.

"Do these money-plus offers represent a good value?"

Occasionally they do. Some manufacturers pass along their volume purchasing savings to you and some even charge less than their cost in order to win your good will. This was the case when wallet-size electronic calculators were first introduced. Several manufacturers offered them for proofs of purchase and a sum of money that was approximately half the store price.

But there are many money-plus offers that aren't really worth the trouble. When the amount of money requested comes close to the store price, it is easier to buy in the store. It is also more convenient to handle returns and repairs through a local store.

Money-plus offers are not considered to be a refund. The forms that advertise money-plus offers are not traded in the way that refund forms are traded. Many refunders consider them to be "junk."

The Refund Form

Most refund offers are made on refund forms. These forms, about the size of a dollar bill, are bound in pads of approximately 100. The pads are usually attached to a supermarket shelf by the manufacturer's salesmen.

On the refund form you will find a place for your name, address, and zip code. You will also find the terms and restrictions of the offer. The Aunt Jemima Free Waffles Offer is a good example of the terms and restrictions you will find on most refund forms:

After the words *"Please Read Carefully,"* you find the term which indicates that the proof of purchase and this form must accompany your request for a refund. The second sentence is a restriction against duplicates or reproductions of the refund form: You can't use a photocopy of the form or anything other than the actual refund form. *"Only one request per name or address"* is a restriction against multiple requests. If the refund requests are kept on a computer which can compare new requests against those already in the computer file, a request by the same named person or from the same address will result in the computer discarding the second request. When this happens some manufacturers will send your request and proofs back to you, but some manufacturers will just discard them without communicating with you. The American Coupon Club believes that every refund request should have a response. Even computers make a mistake and in the case of the offer above, what would happen if several requests came from the same address—an apartment house?

"Group requests will not be honored." This prohibits

a group such as a church from pooling all their refunds and sending them in as a group. This would also prevent several friends from saving postage by sending their refund requests in the same envelope.

"Good only in the U.S.A." prevents our Canadian and Mexican neighbors and other foreigners from sending for refunds. Canadian companies or subsidiaries of U.S. manufacturers make their own coupon and refund offers that are similarly restricted to Canadian residents.

"Void where prohibited, taxed or otherwise restricted," is a catch-all phrase in legal terminology designed to protect the manufacturer in states where such an offer might be prohibited or taxed. It should not affect you the consumer if the offer is advertised or if you find the form in your area.

"Allow six weeks for delivery." In general, it usually takes six to eight weeks before you get your refund in the mail. Be patient!

Most manufacturers use the expiration date to mean that you must have your refund request postmarked no later than this date. It is wise to send it in at least a few days before the offer expires.

Other terms commonly found on refund forms include:

"Limit one per family." This is a restriction similar to that mentioned above for names and addresses.

"Offer good only in areas where product is sold." This is a geographic limitation which means that the manufacturer may not send you the refund if you live outside the area where the product is sold. Many manufacturers don't list specific geographic limitations on the refund form when they test a refund in one area. This causes problems when the refund forms and some of their products stray into other areas. The resulting rejection letters create hard feelings. More thoughtful manufacturers list the states in which their offer is good if they intend to make a geographic restriction.

"Duplicate requests will constitute fraud." This is a strong warning against requesting a second refund when the refund form clearly states "one per family."

"Sale or purchase of this form is prohibited." Such a warning can have no effect upon a refunder. The

refund form becomes your property when you clip it out of the newspaper or tear it off the pad on the supermarket shelf. When it becomes your property you can sell it or transfer it as you please.

Tip from *The Shopper:*

We have known manufacturers who have kept their post office boxes open for several weeks after the expiration date of the refund offer. If you have the refund form and the required proofs and you are a few days late, send it in anyway; your only risk is the postage. If the box is closed the envelope will be returned to you and you won't lose your proofs of purchase.

3

"Where Do I Find Refund Forms?"

You will find refund forms in several places:

- On pads of forms attached to supermarket shelves. By far the greatest number of refund forms are distributed in this way.
- Refund forms are found on the back and inside of specially marked packages. If you look closely at

the packages on the supermarket shelves you will see a great variety of refund offers. Some manufacturers print the refund offers on the backs of labels, others put them on hangtags which are attached to bottles.

• You will find refund forms in newspapers and occasionally in magazines.

"HELP! I can't find enough refund forms"

If you look through several supermarkets in your area and check the weekday food section of your local newspaper you will quickly realize an important fact:

> *These sources will not provide you with enough refund forms.*

"If manufacturers will make more than 7,000 refund offers this year, why don't I see more of their forms in the supermarket?"

This is a good question and here are the answers:

• Some thoughtless stores don't allow the manufacturers' salesmen to put up the pads of refund forms (hopefully this will change as more supermarket executives realize that displaying refund forms actually gives them a competitive advantage with a growing number of refund conscious shoppers).

• A manufacturer's salesman attaches a pad of 100 refund forms to the supermarket shelf and within a day they may all be gone. But this salesman may not return for six to eight weeks to replenish the supply of forms.

• Some greedy shoppers take ten or twenty forms at a time and some even take the whole pad. When I see this happen I tell those shoppers they are being very selfish and ruining refunding for many other people.

Here's How to Get Lots of Refund Forms

Here are the secrets I use to find hundreds of refund forms each month. They help me turn all my boxtops and labels into cash.

• Don't give up hope at the supermarket. I always ask the store manager if he has any refund forms tucked away in a drawer. The manufacturers' salesmen often leave refund forms with the store manager.

Don't forget the cashiers! They may be hiding a few pads of refund forms under the checkout counter just waiting for smart shoppers like you to ask for them.

• Get some help from your family and friends. If they are not refunders they will usually be happy to give you the refund forms they find.

• Put a sign up on your supermarket's bulletin board *"Will Trade Refund Forms."* You should get a lot of calls.

• Start a swap session. It's a fun way to get new forms. Just call some friends and ask them over for coffee. Remind them to bring over their extra coupons and refund forms.

• Coupon clubs are an even better source of refund forms because they draw refunders from a wider area. There can be more trading, more ways to save money, and more fun. Read on—there's a whole chapter on coupon clubs. The A.C.C.'s monthly magazine has a directory of A.C.C. Shopper's Circle coupon clubs. There may be one in your area.

• Experienced refunders trade refund forms by mail. They send out an envelope with twenty refund forms and within a few days they get back an envelope with twenty new forms. The American Coupon Club recommends that its members send out at least two trades a week. You'll find all the details of trading by mail in Chapter 15.

• Writing for forms: It would be wonderful if you could write to a manufacturer for a refund form. You have purchased the product and learned about the refund offer—shouldn't the manufacturer send you a refund form if you request one? The manufacturer should but usually doesn't. A request to Kraft for a refund form brought this response which is fairly typical:

> *"As much as we would like to honor your request for the required mail-in form, we are unable to send it to you. This refund form is available through retail outlets only, therefore, please check with your local retail stores for these forms."*

If manufacturers take the trouble and a 15¢ stamp to respond to your request, we think that they should take a positive step and send you the refund form. Negative replies breed negative feelings and dispel all the good will that has been built up for a good product. But don't despair—read on.

One of the secrets of refunding is that manufacturers do establish special addresses and post office box numbers to handle requests for refund forms. Refunders get this information from the cardboard backing to which store forms are attached. When the last refund form is taken from the pad, the cardboard that remains usually has a notice similar to the one below,

which gives the special address to which you can send your request.

It only takes a postcard to send for a refund form. Be sure that you mention the specific refund offer for which you want a form. Clearly print your name, address, and zip code.

Here is a sample of a typical note you can use to request a refund form:

Please send me a refund form for

THE ALL $2.00 REFUND OFFER

Send it to: Mrs. John Jones
240-11 Fairmont Avenue
Bloomfield Hts., Pa. 17200
Thank You

Patty Jones

Here are a few special addresses to which you can write for forms:
• Baggies Free Sandwich Bag offer, Box 594, Young America, MN 55399 (Send for the form before 5/31/80).
• (S'Mores $1.50 Refund) General Mills, Inc., P.O. Box 96A, Minneapolis, MN 55460. (Offer expires 5/31/80).

• ($1 Gift Cert.) Gentle Touch Gift Certificate Offer, P.O. Box 8355A, Clinton, IA 52736 (Offer expires 5/31/80).

• ($1 Refund) Nabisco Save $1.00, P.O. Box 225, El Paso, TX 79977 (Offer expires 6/30/80).

One of the advantages of joining an organization like the American Coupon Club is that club members share information about where to write for forms. Each month the club's magazine has long lists of these special addresses and box numbers.

Tips from *The Shopper*:

Refund offers made by Procter & Gamble are favorites of experienced refunders. P&G will send you refund forms if you request them, and you can ask for several on one postcard. P&G is a thoughtful company. They will even return your postage when you ask for refund forms. They will also give you an extension slip if the refund offer is close to its expiration date.

When you write to P&G asking for refund forms you must specify each refund offer by its particular name. Merely giving the name of the product is not enough.

To request your refund forms from P&G write to:

Box 432, Cincinnati, OH 45299.

Experienced refunders know that P&G will often give a refund even if they have not sent the refund form. So, if the expiration date draws near and you still haven't found the refund form, send for the refund anyway.

One last P&G tip: They will usually accept proofs of purchase from smaller sizes if they add up to the size required.

Purchasing Refund Forms

If you are just getting started in refunding and re-fund forms are hard to find in your area, you should consider purchasing an initial supply. The classified ad section in *The National Supermarket Shopper* contains ads from experienced refunders who will sell you an assortment of refund forms for a handling fee that is never more than $1.

FOR BEGINNERS. Send 50¢ and SASE and receive 20 good refund forms. Ad good anytime. Sarah Smith, Smithville, DE 00000

NFN—No Form Necessary!

One of the secrets of successful refunding is that some manufacturers will send you a refund even though you don't send them a refund form. This may be true even though the refund form itself says that the form must accompany your request.

Although the majority of refund offers require re-fund forms, a growing number of manufacturers are realizing that despite the best efforts of their salesmen, their refund forms are very hard to find. Rather than create a whole group of customers who are frus-trated and disgruntled because they can't find the form they have heard so much about, these manu-facturers are sending their customers refunds even though the refund form did not accompany the proofs of purchase. One of the objectives of the American Coupon Club is to get more manufacturers to adopt this considerate policy.

"How can I tell which refund offers don't require a refund form?"

The American Coupon Club's magazine, *The National Supermarket Shopper,* lists hundreds of new re-fund offers each month and tells A.C.C. members whether a refund form is required, or if no form is necessary.

You can start refunding right away by checking the refund listings in this book. If you find any that are marked "no form necessary" and you use the products, then you may already have the required proofs of purchase sitting on your kitchen shelf. If you do, just send them to the manufacturer with a brief note asking for the refund.

The editors of *The National Supermarket Shopper* keep careful records of the refund offers of every major manufacturer. A.C.C. club members who receive a refund without a form and those who receive a rejection letter because they did not send a form, pass along this information to the club. Each month the magazine's "Refund Update" column shares this valuable information with all A.C.C. members.

When the editors are in doubt about whether or not an offer requires a form, they mark the offer with a question mark. The question mark is fair warning that you take your chances if you send your proofs of purchase without a refund form.

4

Proofs of Purchase

Your Own Personal Gold Mine

A large collection of boxtops, labels, and other proofs of purchase is just like having your own personal gold mine! With a little work, you can turn all this trash into refund gold.

This is how you work your proof of purchase gold mine:

Every time you find a refund form, or a refund listing that doesn't require a form, you go to your POP gold mine and look for the required boxtops, labels, or other proofs. Once you have a large collection of proofs you will probably find the ones you are looking for ready and waiting for you to cash them into refund gold.

An example of mining for refund gold might work like this: Let's say that your children just can't stop eating Kellogg's cereals. They finish several boxes each week. From now on you are going to save the proof of purchase seals from every box. With the pile of POP seals rapidly building up, you can now start looking for Kellogg's refund offers. Many of them are no form necessary. When you find a good one, you head straight for your POP collection and send for your refund or free product. It's as simple as that.

"What is a proof of purchase?"

If someone asks you that question be careful.

A proof of purchase (POP) can be a boxtop or a universal product code or even the instructions that come inside the package.

A refund offer may ask for any one of several possible proofs of purchase. It can also ask for the cash register tape with the product's purchase price circled.

Here are the most commonly asked-for proofs of purchase:

Proof of Purchase Seal—

A growing number of manufacturers are printing a special proof of purchase seal on their packages to eliminate confusion about the proper proof of purchase. The POP Seal for Golden Grahams cereal is a good example.

Universal Product Code (UPC)—

The thick-and-thin black lines with the numbers below them represent the universal product code found on almost every supermarket product. When a refund offer asks for the UPC code or symbol, be sure to send the numbers as well as the black lines.

Net Weight Statement—

You will usually find the net weight statement (or the fluid ounce statement) on the front of the package, can, or bottle label.

Ingredient Statement—

Manufacturers like Green Giant ask for the ingredient statement as the required proof of purchase. A typical ingredient statement might look like the one below.

INGREDIENTS:
Chicken Broth, Cooked Chicken Meat, Enriched Wheat Flour, Shortening, Rehydrated Potatoes, Carrots, Water, Peas, Chicken Skins, Chicken Fat, Celery, Modified Food Starch, Salt, Margarine, Nonfat Dry Milk, Dextrose, Monosodium Glutamate, Dehydrated Onions, Lactic Acid, Spice, Celery Seeds and Dehydrated Parsley.

Brand Names and Symbols—

A refund offer may ask that you cut out the brand name or product symbol (trademark) which is usually found printed on the front of the package. The symbol of Aunt Jemima has been well known for decades. The Jell-O brand name is well known and easily recognized.

Boxtops and Box Bottoms—

There are still many manufacturers who ask for the boxtop as their proof of purchase. You must send the whole boxtop and not just a part of it. Occasionally a refund offer, like a recent one from Cheerios, may ask for the box bottom.

Price Spot—

Many packages have a round price spot in which the grocer stamps the price of the item. This is occasionally asked for as a proof of purchase.

Side Panel—

Almost every box has two side panels. Manufacturers may ask for a side panel and then designate one of them by telling you that they want the one with the cooking directions or the nutritional information statement.

Send The Words "————"

Some refunds ask that you cut out and send as your proof of purchase certain words that may appear on the package. The directions on the refund form may state: "Send the words 'Colgate-Palmolive' from the side panels of two boxes of . . ." Or the offer may ask for the portion of the box or wrapper that says "Tear Strip" or "Open Here" or "Pull-Up."

Cash Register Tapes—

Almost a quarter of the refund offers require a cash register tape or a sales receipt as additional proof of purchase.

The manufacturer's refund offer asks you to send a POP from their product plus the cash register tape with the price of the product circled.

Because of this requirement, most refunders regularly save all their cash register tapes just as they save all their package POPs. When they need a tape they will have it handy.

When you are buying a specific item for a refund offer, circle the price as soon as you get home.

Identifying a specific purchase on a tape that is several weeks old can be a bit of a problem, but most refunders are able to work it out.

What do you do if you have to make several purchases that each require a register tape? One thing you can do is to shop at a time when the store isn't crowded and ask the cashier to ring up these few items on separate tapes. One thing that you can't do is to cut up one tape for several proofs.

Identifying an item on a register tape will become a lot easier when the stores convert to electronic computer-controlled cash registers. These registers print the brand name of each of your purchases right on the register tape.

Guarantees, Instructions, Etc., Etc.

A smart refunder will also save items like guarantees and instruction sheets. A recent refund offer from

No-Nonsense Pantyhose asked for the "No-Nonsense Guarantee," while a second offer asked for the size chart from the back of the package, and a third offer asked for the rear pouch flaps. A refund offer from o.b. Tampons asked for the instruction leaflet packed inside each box.

"What POPs should I save?"

Do you want to shoot for the big savings?

If you do, then you should try to save *everything!* This requires that you save almost every proof of purchase listed above from every branded product you use.

There are three important reasons for saving everything:

• Manufacturers often change their proof of purchase requirements. A manufacturer who has always asked for boxtops suddenly changes to UPC codes, and there you sit with eighteen boxtops which you had stashed away for that next big $5 refund. How sad!

• Manufacturers often ask for different proofs at different times and for different offers. They may ask for the net weight statement for a $2 refund and the following month ask for the picture of the baby on the front of the package for a free product offer.

Does this mean that you can get the proofs needed for two refunds from one package?

You certainly can! And you would be surprised how often this happens. In some cases refunders have gotten as many as three refunds from the proofs from one box.

• Manufacturers are making more tie-in offers that ask for a POP from their product plus a POP from any brand of another type of product usually associated with their own. For instance, a coffee producer may ask for a POP from any brand of cake, pastry, or dessert. A POP from Aunt Jemima Frozen Waffles was asked for along with a POP from any brand of frozen orange juice.

Last Fall several manufacturers had tie-in refund offers that also asked for proofs of purchase from a turkey. One offer asked for the name of the turkey, another asked for a yellow oval from a specific branded turkey, and a third asked for the weight and price label. A fourth asked for cooking directions from the turkey wrapper. I received four refunds with proofs from one turkey.

"But I can't save everything, I live in an apartment!"

Saving *everything* does require a lot of space. Many refunders have an entire room, or a major part of their basement or garage, filled with proofs of purchase.

For new refunders and those with limited space, I suggest that you use the following list of most commonly asked-for proofs of purchase. We have taken our list of manufacturers who frequently make refund offers and we have listed the types of proofs that they have asked for during the past year.

This is not meant to be a complete listing, and it should be understood that manufacturers are continously changing their POP requirements. Just because the last offer we saw from Cheerios asked for the box bottom does not mean that they can't change their requirement to the net weight statement tomorrow.

A helpful note: Along with the name of the manufacturer, we list the address of the company's principal office and the name of the president or executive in charge of customer relations. If you have a problem which the customer relations department does not resolve to your satisfaction, the president of the company would probably be interested in learning about it.

A Beginner's POP List

When it comes to proofs of purchase, we advise all refunders to SAVE EVERYTHING! But some beginners would rather start slowly and collect only those proofs they know manufacturers want. There are also refunders who live in apartments and don't have sufficient room to build up a large POP collection. For these beginners and apartment dwellers we have put together a list of required proofs of purchase.

When using this beginners POP list, several things should be carefully remembered: First, it is only a partial list of manufacturers and products. We don't have enough space to list the more than 1,000 manufacturers who make refund offers. Second, the proofs listed were those required *last year,* and this doesn't mean that the manufacturer isn't going to change the proofs required for this year's offers—it happens often. Our listing may say that the required proof is a boxtop and next month the manufacturer may put out a new refund offer that requires a box bottom! So . . . the only way to be absolutely certain that you aren't throwing out proofs that will be required in the future is to *save everything*.

Our POP listings also contain information that can be used to communicate with the manufacturers. You will find the manufacturer's address and in most cases the name of the person in charge of customer relations. If a complaint is not handled satisfactorily by the customer relations department, you may want to write directly to the president of the company.

AMERICAN BRANDS, INC., 245 Park Avenue., New York, NY 10017
(212-557-9000).
President: J.F. Walrath
Consumer Relations: May Roy (Duffy Mott), A. Byra (Sunshine)

Sunshine—Proof of purchase seals
Duffy Mott—Ingredient panels, Quality seals

ARMOUR AND CO., Greyhound Tower, Phoenix, AZ
85077
(602-248-2000)
President: D.J. Shaughnessy
Director of Consumer Service: Dott McGill

Armour Star—complete labels
Armour Dial—Fluid oz. wt. statement

BEATRICE FOODS CO., 2 North La Salle, Chicago,
IL 60602
(312-782-3820)
President: D.P. Eckrich
Director of Public Relations: Peter Vandernoot

Aunt Nellie's—Complete labels
Dannon—Net wt. statement
La Choy—Bottom can labels

BORDEN INC., 277 Park Ave., New York, NY 10017
(212-573-4000) Or (614-225-4511) COLLECT for
complaints.
President: E.J. Sullivan

Borden—Proof of purchase seals
Borden Cheese—Labels
Cremora—Net wt. statement
Lite-Line—Front panel
Wyler's—Complete labels

BRISTOL MYERS CO., 345 Park Ave., New York,
NY 10022
(212-644-2100)
President: H. Sokol
Consumer Relations: Edna Dambra (Bristol Myers),
Guillian Hee (Clairol)

Bristol Myers—Front labels
Clairol—Front labels/panels

BUITONI FOODS CORPORATION, 450 Huyler St.,
South Hackensack, NJ 07606
(201-440-8000)
President: M. Buitoni

Quality Control: Mitchell Feingold

Buitoni—Net wt. statement or front label

CAMPBELL SOUP CO., Campbell Place, Camden, NJ
08101
(609-964-4000)
President: H.A. Shaub
Consumer Services: D. Robinson

Campbell—Front labels
Franco American—UPC codes
Pepperidge Farm—Price marks
Swanson—Front variety panel

CARNATION CO., 5045 Wilshire Blvd., Los Angeles,
CA 90036
(213-931-1911)
President: D.L. Stuart
Consumer Relations: L. Abranson

Mighty Dog—Front labels
Carnation—UPC code
Coffee Mate—Front labels

CASTLE AND COOKE, INC., 50 California St., San
Francisco, CA 94111
(415-986-3000)
President: D.J. Kirchnoff
Director of Consumer Services: R. Hubbard

Bumble Bee—Front labels
Dole—Label

CELENTANO BROS., 225 Bloomfield Ave., Verona,
NJ 07044
(201-239-8444)
President: D. Celentano
Consumer Relations: D. Celentano

Celentano's—Side panels with "Celentano"

COCA-COLA CO., Foods Division, Katy Rd., Houston, TX 77055

(713-868-8100)
President: I. Herbert
Consumer Relations: Mary J. Dann

Hi-C—Quality seals
Minute Maid—Opening strips
Snow Crop—Opening strips

COLGATE-PALMOLIVE CO., 300 Park Ave., New
York, NY 10022
(212-751-1200)
President: K. Crane
Manager of Consumer Affairs: K. Fitzsimmons

Ajax—Net wt. markings or fl. oz. markings
Baggies—Words "Colgate Palmolive Co."
Colgate—ADA seals and net wt. statements
Cold Power—Box tops
Fab—Boxtop
Handi Wipes—Green seal "8 reusable cloths"
Irish Spring—Wrapper
Palmolive—Net. wt. statement

N. DORMAN AND CO., INC., 125 Michael Dr.,
Syosset, NY 11791
(516-364-1600)
President: A. Dorman
Consumer Affairs: B. Grasso

Dorman's—Package fronts

FRITO-LAY INC., Frito-Lay Tower, Dallas, TX
75235
(214-351-7000)
President: D. Calloway
Manager of Consumer Services: G. Thomason

Fritos—Net wt. statements
Chitos—Net wt. statements
Lays—Net wt. statements

GENERAL FOODS CORP., 250 North St., White
Plains, NY 10625
(914-683-2500)

President: R. Barzelay
Manager of Consumer Response: Barbara Whitney

Bac'Os—Freshness seal
Birds Eye—Tear strips
Jello—Boxtops
Kool Aid—Envelopes
Maxwell House—Inner seal
Minute Rice—Boxtops
Sanka—Empty envelopes
Shake 'n Bake—Empty envelopes

GENERAL MILLS CO., 9200 Wayzata Blvd., Minneapolis, MN 55440
(612-540-2311)
President: H.B. Atwater, Jr.
Director of Sales Administration: W. LeSueur

Betty Crocker—Box bottom panels
Cereals (Cheerios, Wheaties, Total . . .)—Boxtops or bottoms
Gorton's—Proof of purchase symbol
Hamburger Helper—Box bottoms

GILLETTE CO., Prudential Tower Bldg., Boston, MA. 02199
(617-421-7000)
President: S.J. Griffin
Vice President of Public Relations: D. Fausch

Gillette—Proof of purchase seal

GREEN GIANT CO., Hazeltine Gates, Chaska, MN 55318
(612-665-3515)
President: T. Wyman
Manager of Consumer Affairs: Mary Jenks

Green Giant—Ingredient statements
Le Sueur—Labels

H.J. HEINZ CO., 1062 Progress St., Pittsburgh, PA 15212

(412-237-5757)
President: A.J. O'Reilly
Consumer Relations: F. Shoemaker

Heinz—Labels
9-lives—Labels
Star Kist—Labels

HERSHEY'S FOOD CORP., 19 E. Chocolate Ave.,
Hershey, PA 17033
(717-534-4200)
President: R.A. Zimmerman
Consumer Information: J.A. Bianchini

Hershey's—Net wt. statements
Skinner's—Cooking instructions

HUNT WESSON FOODS INC., 1645 W. Valencia Dr.,
Fullerton, CA 92634
(714-871-2100)
President: W. Hood
Consumer Relations: L. King

Hunt's—Neck bands or can labels
Wesson—Labels

KEEBLER CO., One Hollow Tree La., Elmhurst, IL
60126
(312-833-2900)
President: T. Garvin
Director of Customer Relations: J. Peters

Keebler—Proof of purchase stickers
Townhouse—Proof of purchase stickers

KELLOGG CO., 235 Porter St., Battle Creek, MI
49016
(616-966-2000)
President: W.E. LaMathe
Consumer Relations: Muriel Cleary

Kellogg's—Boxtops
Mrs. Smith's—UPC code

KIMBERLY-CLARK CORP., Neenah, WI 54956
(414-729-1212)
President: R.C. Ernest
Consumer Relations: D. Stobaugh

Boutique—Product code symbols
Delsey—Product code symbols
Kleenex—Product code symbols

KRAFT, INC., 500 N. Peshtigo Ct., Chicago, IL 60690
(312-222-4600)
President: A.W. Woelfle
Manager of Consumer Services: S. Victors

Breakstone—Product code symbols
Catalina—Product code symbols
Miracle Whip—Product code symbols
Light & Lively—Product code symbols
Sealtest—Proof of purchase seal

LEVER BROS., 390 Park Ave., New York, NY 10022
(212-688-6000)
President: T. Carroll
Manager of Consumer Services: Ann Ryan

Aim—Panel with "Lever Bros."
Closeup—Net wt. statements
Dove—Labels
Lux—Net wt. statement
Signal—Fluid oz. statement on label

LIBBY, MCNEILL & LIBBY CO., 1700 W. 119 St.,
Chicago, IL 60643
(313-341-4111)
President: I. Murray
Consumer Relations: Cathy Goles

Libby's—Labels

THOMAS LIPTON INC., 800 Sylvan Ave., Englewood Cliffs, NJ 07632
(201-567-8000)
President: H. Tibbetts
Manager of Consumer Affairs: Marie McDermott

Lipton—Front panels
Morton House—Labels
Wishbone—Neck bands

MCNEIL CONSUMER PRODUCTS CO., Camp Hill
Rd., Port Washington, PA 19034
(215-836-4500)
President: W. Nelson
Consumer Affairs: Carla L. Cote

Tylenol—Front labels/panels

MUELLER CO., 180 Baldwin Ave., Jersey City, NJ
07306
(201-653-3800)
President: L. Thurston
Director of Technical Services: V. Bremer

Mueller's—Product code symbols or front panels

NABISCO, INC., East Hanover, NJ 07936
(201-884-0500)
President: V.B. Diehl
Manager of Consumer Services: M. Lehy

Milk Bone—Purchase confirmation seals
Premium—Proof of purchase seal
Ritz—Proof of purchase seal

OSCAR MAYER & CO., INC., 910 Mayer Ave.,
Madison, WI 53704
(608-241-6825)
President: J. Hiegel
Customer Relations: J. Bolz

Oscar Mayer—Front flap labels

PILLSBURY CO., 608 Second Ave., Minneapolis, MN
55402
(612-330-4966)
President: W.R. Wallin
Vice President of Consumer Affairs: M.E. Jenks

Hungry Jack—Boxtops
Pillsbury—Labels

PROCTER & GAMBLE CO., 301 E. 6th St., Cincinnati, OH 45202
(513-562-1100)
President: J.G. Smale
Consumer Relations: C.M. Fullgraf, Manager (paper products), C.C. Carroll, Manager (toilet products)

Bounty—"To open pull up" from package
Charmin—Picture of baby
Coast—Wrapper
Duncan Hines—Net wt. statement
Folger's—Jar/inner seal, can/plastic lid
Ivory—Fluid oz. statement
Pampers—Picture of baby
Pringles—Nt. wt. statement from plastic wrapper
Tide—Net wt. statement
White Cloud—"To open pull up" from package

QUAKER OATS CO., Merchandise Mart Plaza, Chicago, IL 60654
(312-222-7111)
President: K. Mason
Vice President of Consumer Services: Lois I. Ross

Aunt Jemima—Ingredient statements
Celeste—Net wt. statement
Cereals (Captain Crunch, Life)—Seals when available or boxtops.
Flako—Proof of purchase seal

RAGU FOODS INC. 1680, Lyell Ave., Rochester, NY 14606
(716-458-0886)
President: C. Chapman
Consumer Services: (33 Benedict Pl., Greenwich, CT 06830) Ann Dedona

Ragù—Labels
Adolph's—Labels

RALSTON PURINA CO., 835 S. 8th St., St. Louis, MO 63188
(314-982-1000)

President: R.H. Dean
Manager of Consumer Relations: Doris Hewkin

Purina—Labels
Chicken of the Sea—Labels

R.J. REYNOLDS FOODS INC., R.J.R. World Head-
quarters, Reynolds Bldg., Winston Salem, NC 27102
(919-777-4300)
President: J.B. Sticht
Public Relations: P. Allan

Chun King—Net wt. statements
Del Monte—Del Monte shields
Hawaiian Punch—Front label
Vermont Maid Syrup—Labels

KITCHENS OF SARA LEE Inc., 500 Waukegan Rd.,
Deerfield, IL 60015
(312-945-2525)
President: L.M. Beggs
Consumer Relations: Barbara McDonald

Sara Lee—Ingredient statements

SCOTT PAPER CO., Scott Plaza, Philadelphia, PA
19113
(215-521-5000)
President: M.V. Hunter
Consumer Relations: Janet Jones

Cottenelle—Seals of quality
Scott—Seals of quality
Viva—Seals of quality

SMUCKER & CO., Strawberry La., Orrville, OH
44667
(216-602-0015)
President: P.H. Smucker
Customer Relations: Vicki Wanner

Smucker's—Full lable or net wt. statements

STANDARD BRANDS INC., 625 Madison Ave., New York, NY 11022
  (212-759-4400)
  President: O.L. Applegate
  Consumer Affairs: Mary Anne Woods

  Planter's—Inner seal
  Curtis Candy (Baby Ruth, Butterfinger, Reggie)—Wrapper
  Royal—Front panels
  Crackerjax—Nutritional information panels

WEIGHT WATCHER'S INTERNATIONAL INC., 800 Community Dr., Manhasset, NY 11030
  (516-627-9200)
  President: C. Berger
  Consumer Complaints: Cheryl Tyree

  Weight Watcher's—Top panels

WELCH FOODS INC., Westfield, NY 14787
  (716-326-3131)
  President: T. Whitney
  Consumer Relations: J. Weidman III

  Welch's—Net wt. statements

Organizing Your POP Collection

Most refunders organize their POP collection either by product group or alphabetically by name of product or manufacturer, whichever is better known. Both methods work equally well.

I separate my POPs into the twelve A.C.C. product groups (you will find them listed on page 61). I have a carton for each group, and in each carton I arrange the proofs alphabetically.

Each carton has an envelope for the smaller POPs such as POP seals. It keeps them from getting lost among the larger folded packages.

When you start your POP collection you can keep your POPs in large envelopes or shoe boxes. As your collection grows you will probably graduate to corrugated shipping cartons as I have.

Tips from *The Shopper:*

Here are some valuable tips that will help you with your POP collection:

- Save space by peeling the label from the cardboard behind it.
- When you are saving everything it is often easier to fold the whole package flat instead of cutting out all the POPs.
- Keep your growing collection of POPs out of sight and out of the way of other members of the family.
- Carefully clean your POPs before filing them.
- When you cut out a POP such as a net weight statement or a UPC code, be sure to write the product's name on the back. They are worthless if you don't know where they came from.
- Keep a single carton in your kitchen to hold the packages, cans, and bottles from which you will later remove the POPs. When the carton is filled, then it is time for cutting, cleaning, and filing.
- Try to save everything—the POP you save today may bring you a $2 refund next week, next month, or next year.

5

Sending for Your Refunds

Sending for your refund is relatively simple, but there are a few things that you should be aware of:

Sending for "No Form Necessary" Refunds

When a manufacturer doesn't require a refund form, you can send your proofs of purchase clipped to a simple note like this:

> Dear Sirs:
> Enclosed you will find three neck bands from Smith's Bugle Dressings. Please send the Smith's Bugle $2 Refund to:
> > Jane Jones
> > 4 Jones Street
> > Jonesville, IL 61472

Even if the manufacturer doesn't require a form, if you have it, you should always use it.

Sending for a Form-Required Offer

When a refund form is required, all you have to do is fill out the spaces on the form, follow the requirements carefully, and send it to the address of the offer along with your proofs of purchase. Be sure to fill in the blank spaces as clearly as possible. Typing is best, but if you don't have a typewriter, make sure to print your name, address and zip code as clearly as possible.

"What should I do when I have the required proofs, the expiration date is drawing near, and I still can't find the required form?"

If you know that a form is definitely required, it is a waste of 15¢, an envelope, and your time to send for the refund without it. But, if you aren't certain whether a form is required, and with some manufacturers it is hard to be certain, you may want to risk the postage and take a chance. If you do send for the refund without the form, include a note such as this one:

Dear Sirs:

Enclosed are the 3 neck bands required for the Smith's Bugle $2 Refund.

My supermarket ran out of your refund form and although I have searched everywhere, I have not been able to find one. I enjoy Smith's Bugle Dressings and would appreciate receiving this refund.

Sincerely yours,

Jane Jones
41 Jones Street
Jonesville, IL 61472

Tip from *The Shopper*:

Inexpensive name and address labels are available from a variety of sources. You can buy 500 for as little as a dollar or two. The self-adhesive kind is best. Pasting an address label to a refund form saves you time and ensures that the form will be easily read at the refund clearing house. When you become an avid refunder, these labels really come in handy.

"Can you send for a refund offer a few days after it expires?"

The best policy is to send in your refund request a few days *before* it expires. Some companies do instruct their clearing house to accept refund requests for a brief period after the expiration date. But this isn't something that you can depend on. What should you do if you wake up on a Monday and remember the offer that expired on Friday? If you send it, you risk 15¢ postage and you take your chances.

"Box Closed"

When you receive your refund request envelope back with "Box Closed" stamped across the manufacturer's address, the chances are that you sent your request in after the expiration date, or the offer may have had no expiration date, and the manufacturer finally decided to close the offer.

The refund clearing houses employed by the manufacturers have so many different box numbers that they occasionally close one by mistake. If this happens, complain directly to the manufacturer.

Rejection Letters

Even experienced refunders receive rejection letters. So, you shouldn't be disturbed when you receive your first rejection letter. It's all part of the game.

Some of the most common reasons for receiving a rejection letter are as follows:

• You submitted your request without the required refund form.
• You do not live within the geographic area to which the refund offer was limited. (Most considerate manufacturers who limit their offers to specific states, print these limitations right on the refund form. Those that don't, create a great deal of ill will and lose many of their best customers.)
• You did not include the proper proofs (you may have included the wrong size) or the proper number of proofs.

- You may have inadvertently submitted a second request for the same refund offer when the offer was limited to one per family or address.
- The offer has expired.

Here is a typical rejection letter:

Dear Consumer:

We regret that it is not possible for us to send your refund to you at the present time.

Through some misunderstanding or oversight you did not fulfill our requirements as stated in our advertising to which you responded.

In order to be fair to all the thousands of people who have replied to our offer, we must limit the refund to those in full compliance with the respective offer.

YOUR REQUEST IS BEING RETURNED FOR THE FOLLOWING REASONS. PLEASE RESUBMIT IN THE PROPER MANNER.

    X   Original name and address form was not enclosed.
    _____ Cash register tape not enclosed.
    _____ No labels enclosed.
    _____ Incorrect labels enclosed.
    _____ Incorrect number of labels enclosed.
    _____ Improper proof of purchase.
    _____ Other.

PLEASE DO NOT RESUBMIT YOUR REQUEST IF IT HAS BEEN RETURNED FOR ANY OF THE FOLLOWING REASONS:
    _____ Duplicate request. Offer limited to one per family or address.
    _____ Offer expired.
    _____ Other.

Some thoughtful manufacturers now include some cashoff coupons with their rejection letters!

Refunding Requires Patience

One of the hardest parts of refunding is waiting for the refund to appear in your mailbox. Unfortunately, most manufacturers and their clearing houses take from six to eight weeks to send refunds.

Some refunders find it irritating to wait for months to receive refunds. Many manufacturers don't realize that they lose a lot of the goodwill produced by the refund when shoppers wait and wait to receive it.

But you must wait and be patient. Wait ten weeks

for your refund. If you still haven't received it at the end of this period, it is time to complain.

Refund Offer Complaints

Experience has shown that the best way to get action when you have a refund offer complaint is to write directly to the manufacturer's customer relations department. Don't write to the same address as the one to which you sent your refund request.

You can find the manufacturer's address on the product package. Even if the address is just a city and a zip code, don't worry, it will get there.

When you complain about not receiving a refund, that your request was wrongfully rejected, be sure that you clearly state the facts. Explain the situation completely. When you have finished the letter, read it over carefully, and make certain that even a person unfamiliar with the situation can understand it.

Tips from *The Shopper*—To Manufacturers:

Some manufacturers are very considerate of their customers and treat their refund requests in a way that builds goodwill and product loyalty. Here are some of the ways that they do it:

• If a refund offer has a geographic limitation, they print it on the refund form. (Shoppers often live on the edge of the area in which a refund is promoted but outside the geographic limitations of the offer.)

• They print expiration dates on all their refund forms so that shoppers don't have to guess whether offers are still valid.

• If they publicize a refund offer with the knowledge that only a small percentage of their customers will be able to find the refund forms, then they also publicize a special address where the form can be obtained, or instruct their clearing house to accept the proofs without the refund form.

(Unfortunately, there are many manufacturers who spend millions for promotions but aren't thoughtful in many of the small ways that really count. They wonder why they have to send out so many rejection letters and why their customers switch to other brands.)

• There are circumstances where a rejection letter is warranted. Small manufacturers turn it to their advantage by sending a few cashoff coupons along with the rejection letter. This is usually a pleasant surprise to the customer; it keeps their loyalty and generates new sales.

• Manufacturers do everything within their power to get the refunds back to their customers within 30 days.

(Manufacturers who don't believe that their customers count the days are wrong! After four weeks, customers become irritated. After six weeks, they become angry. At the eight-week point, they send out a complaint letter and often switch brands.)

The Mail at the End of the Refund Rainbow

Here are examples of the refunds that will fill your mailbox with supermarket savings if you follow this guide:

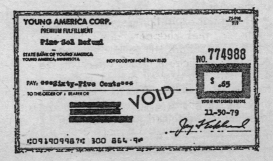

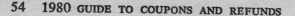

STORE COUPON
GET IT AT YOUR GROCER'S

ONE DOLLAR CERTIFICATE

114024

ONE

Good ONLY toward the purchase of any Fresh Fruit and/or your favorite Kellogg's cereal.

Certificate valid when signed on above line and redeemed before August 31, 1980.
NOT REDEEMABLE FOR CASH

ONE

VOID

FREE   **FREE**

This coupon is good for
ONE FREE POUND of
Mrs. Filbert's Golden Quarters Margarine

MrsFilberts

VOID

STORE COUPON

FREE   **FREE**

FREE   STORE COUPON   **FREE**

FREE Quart of Orange Juice

VOID

560941

(or 12 oz. can of orange juice concentrate)
from the makers of Taster's Choice®
100% Freeze-Dried Coffee and Total® Cereal.

560941

FREE   COUPON MUST BE REDEEMED BEFORE JUNE 1, 1979.   **FREE**

STORE COUPON

FREE   52-A

Present La Crosta Pizza Crust Mix and
coupon together at checkout counter.

FREE LA CROSTA PIZZA CRUST MIX

LA CROSTA
CRUST MIX

52-A   **FREE**

EXPIRES DECEMBER 31, 1979

MULTIFOODS.

STORE COUPON

Good for One Free Can of Green Giant Brand SWEET PEAS

GREEN GIANT

SWEET PEAS

VOID

DEALER: You are authorized as our agent to allow this customer one (1) free can of Green Giant Brand Sweet Peas.

INDICATE PURCHASE PRICE ON BACK OF THIS COUPON

18-499

Refund Request Needed

Use this record sheet to keep track of your refund requests.

REFUND REQUEST RECORD

Name of Refund/ Address	Number of Proofs Sent	Date Sent	Date Rec'd.	Amt./ Value Rec'd.

REFUND REQUEST RECORD

Name of Refund/ Address	Number of Proofs Sent	Date Sent	Date Rec'd.	Amt./ Value Rec'd.

6

Cashing In on Cashoff Coupons

Are you getting your fair share of savings from manufacturers' cashoff coupons?

What is your fair share? About $300 to $400 each year. Even more if stores in your area are promoting their business with double value coupons.

If you didn't save that much in 1979 don't fret. Manufacturers are distributing more coupons every year and they will help you make up for it. This year they

will give out more than 80 billion cashoff coupons. That's right, 80 BILLION!

So, if you want to be a big winner at the coupon game, follow this chapter carefully. It will show you how to find, organize and use all this "coupon currency."

Coupons Are Easy to Find

In just a few short months you can build up an inventory of hundreds of cashoff coupons. Here are some of the places to look:

• The best place to find manufacturers' cashoff coupons is in the food section of your daily newspaper. The food section usually appears on a Wednesday or a Thursday depending on what part of the country you live in. Each week this newspaper is one of your best shopping investments. It is not unusual to find coupons worth $5 or more in a newspaper that costs you a quarter.

If you live in an area where there is no daily newspaper or there are few advertisements containing coupons, arrange with your local newspaper dealer or distributor to get the food day newspapers from nearby cities.

- You will find cashoff coupons in homemaker magazines such as *Family Circle, Woman's Day, Better Homes and Gardens, Good Housekeeping, Redbook* and *McCall's*. There are usually enough cashoff coupons and refunds in these magazines to more than pay for their cost.
- You will find lots of cashoff coupons on the back and inside of specially marked packages. We call these packages SMPs for short. We will tell you more about them in the chapter on supermarket shopping.
- Many shoppers receive coupons in the mail such as the Carol Wright package of coupons. The Carol Wright packages are periodically mailed to more than twenty million households.
- Many thoughtful supermarkets have a coupon exchange box where you can drop in a few coupons you don't need and take out a few useful ones.
- You will also find new coupons at swap sessions and coupon club meetings. You will read all about it in the chapter on coupon clubs.

Cashoff coupons are usually good for many months; like refund forms, some have no expiration date. If you look for them and clip out everything you find, you will soon have a very large inventory. I usually have as many as 2,000 to select from.

Tip from *The Shopper*:
Save every cashoff coupon you find even though you don't use the product. You will be able to trade the coupons you can't use for others that are of value to you.

"How much can I save with cashoff coupons?"

This year, the average cashoff coupon discount will be approximately 16 percent. This is greater than the rate of supermarket inflation! Some coupons, especially those for new products, will give you discounts of 20 percent to 30 percent and more.

A cashoff coupon will mean a lot more to you if you know the percent of discount it gives you. For instance, a 10¢-off coupon doesn't sound like much, but it means more to you when you know that on a 50¢ item, it will give you a discount of 20 percent. Don't you wish that you could get 20 percent off on all your purchases, or get $2 back for every $10 you spend?

Because most shoppers don't walk down the supermarket aisles with an electronic calculator, the American Coupon Club provides its members with a monthly survey of typical cashoff coupons and the important discounts they provide. Here is an example of a coupon survey that appeared in the club's magazine last fall:

November Cashoff Coupon Survey:

This month a total of 28 cashoffs were surveyed. The average discount was 17.4% of the retail price. Discounts ranged from a high of 52% for a can of Kal Kan Dog Food to a low of 5% for a bottle of Tylenol Extra Strength Tablets. The percent of discount may vary depending on the store and part of the country in which the product is purchased. Products with a discount of 20% or more are indicated with an asterisk (*).

File #	Manufacturer/Product	Size	Retail Price	Cashoff Coupon	Percent Discount
1	Downflake Jumbo Frozen Waffles	16 pack	.69	7 cents	10%
1	Kellogg's Frosted Mini-Wheats	14 oz.	1.13	12 cents	9%
2	Borden's American Single Slices	12 slices	1.09	15 cents	14%
2	Diet Imperial Imitation Margarine		.79	10 cents	13%
3*	Nestle Souptime Instant Soups		.49	12 cents	24%
3	Wise Potato Chips		.79	10 cents	13%
3*	Kellogg's Pop-Tarts		.59	15 cents	25%
4	Del Monte Pineapple Chunks	20 oz.	.67	10 cents	14%
4	Comstock Pie Filling/Apple		.75	10 cents	13%
4*	Mueller's Spaghetti	16 oz.	.39	10 cents	25%
5*	Adolph's Meat Marinade		.35	15 cents	43%
5	Yoo-Hoo Chocolate Flavored Syrup	22 oz.	.99	10 cents	10%
5	Domino Granulated Sugar	2 lbs.	.69	10 cents	14%
6	Chicken of the Sea Tuna	6½ oz.	.65	7 cents	11%
6*	Wilson's Western Style Smoked Sausage	15 oz.	1.75	40 cents	22%
6	Van de Kamp's Fish Fillets	14 oz.	2.19	35 cents	16%
7	4 C Bread Crumbs	45 oz.	.73	8 cents	11%
7	Mrs. Smith's Frozen Pumpkin Custard Pie		1.89	15 cents	8%
8	Maxim Freeze-Dried Coffee	4 oz.	2.85	40 cents	14%
8*	Sacramento Tomato Juice	46 oz.	.50	15 cents	25%
9	ReaLemon Reconstituted Lemon Juice	16 oz.	.59	10 cents	17%
9	Fruitcrest Wild Strawberry Preserves	24 oz.	1.00	10 cents	10%
10	Dermassage Dishwashing Liquid	22 oz.	.99	10 cents	10%
10*	Yes Laundry Detergent	32 oz.	1.39	30 cents	22%
11-A	Tylenol Extra Strength Tablets		2.99	15 cents	5%
11-B	Crest	8 oz.	1.05	10 cents	10%
12-B*	Kal Kan Dog Food		.29	15 cents	52%
12-B*	Good Mews Cat Food	16 oz.	.39	15 cents	32%

"Coupon Mess"

Most coupon clippers suffer from "coupon mess"!

Coupon mess is a sickness of sorts. It robs shoppers of the pleasure of big coupon savings. They catch coupon mess when they throw all their cashoff coupons into a drawer or a shoebox. There they usually accumulate and after a while the following symptoms appear:

• It takes twenty minutes to rummage through the pile of coupons to find the 10¢-off coupon they are looking for—who has the patience?

• Coupons that are on the bottom of the pile are forgotten and shoppers wind up buying the products without the discount.

• They don't notice that some of the coupons have expired and they are embarrassed when the cashier throws the expired coupons back at them.

If you have any of these symptoms, then you too could be suffering from coupon mess!

But don't call an ambulance or a carpenter to build new drawers in your kitchen, there is a cure.

Organize your cashoff coupons into twelve easy-to-use product groups. These are the same product groups in which I list all my refund offers.

Cashoff Coupon Product Groups

1. Cereals, Breakfast Products, Baby Products
2. Dairy Products, Oils, Margarine, Diet Products
3. Soups, Snack Foods, Candy
4. Vegetables, Starches, Fruits
5. Seasonings, Sauces, Sugar, Syrups, Salad Dressings
6. Meat, Poultry, Seafood, Other Main Dishes
7. Baked Goods, Desserts
8. Beverages
9. Miscellaneous Food Products
10. Cleaning Products, Soaps, Paper Products, Bags, Wraps

11. Health Aids, Personal Products, Cosmetics
12. Miscellaneous Non-Food Products, Pet
    Products, Tobacco

After you have separated your cashoff coupons into these groups, you can keep them in twelve envelopes or file folders, or a large twelve section portfolio-style organizer.

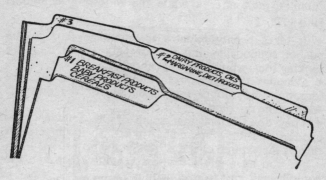

Cleaning Your Coupon Files

Most cashoff coupons expire on the last day of the month. I make it a habit to go through all my coupon files around the twentieth of the month and remove those that are about to expire. This gives me ten days to use those coupons that are still worth taking advantage of, and I put them right into my coupon wallet.

Coupon Wallets

Every couponer should use a coupon wallet.

A good coupon wallet makes it easier to handle your coupons at the supermarket. But, you shouldn't try to keep your whole coupon collection in a wallet. Nor should you allow coupons left over from past shopping trips to accumulate in your wallet. Before each trip to the supermarket, empty your coupon wallet and get a fresh start.

Coupon wallets come in a variety of sizes and styles. In addition to holding your coupons on your trip to the supermarket, the wallet can be used to separate those coupons for products which you have already taken off the shelves from those which you have not as yet found. As you pick up each coupon product, find its coupon and move it from one side of the wallet to the other. When you have finished selecting your purchases, all the coupons you will need for the cashier will be ready on one side of your wallet.

"Why do manufacturers distribute cashoff coupons?"

Coupons help to sell products! Manufacturers of food and household products have found that cashoff coupons are one of their most effective sales devices. Coupons are used to push the sales of new products, to revitalize the sales of old products, and to counteract the sales efforts of competing manufacturers.

A manufacturer introducing a new supermarket product wants to get it into as many homes as quickly as possible. It is the manufacturer's hope that the new product will be liked and that word-of-mouth will reinforce the introductory advertising program. Manufacturers know that a cashoff coupon is one of the most effective methods to move products quickly from the supermarket shelf to the kitchen table. Statistics show that during the month following the distribution of a cashoff coupon, sales can increase on the order of 300 to 400 percent!

A manufacturer can also use cashoff coupons to fight new competition. Here is an example:

Manufacturer X who has a strong market position in Florida learns that a competitor plans to introduce a similar product in the Florida market.

What can manufacturer X do to fight this new competition?

Manufacturer X's marketing department suggests that X brand cashoff coupons be quickly placed in all the major Florida newspapers before the competitor's advertising campaign begins. X's strategy is to load up every household with a large supply of product X, so that when the competitor's products reach the stores there will be few shoppers interested in buying it.

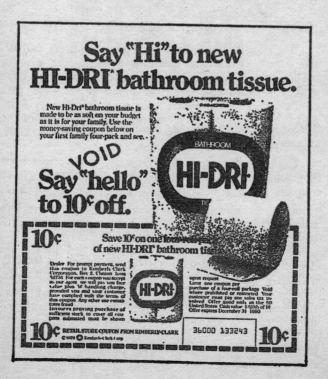

The next time you open the daily newspaper and start clipping coupons, you will know that there is an important marketing strategy behind each of them.

"Is it possible that manufacturers will stop distributing coupons?"

Not in the forseeable future. Our country is blessed with an overabundance of food. As long as this continues, there will be strong competition among the various manufacturers. They will use coupons whenever they find an opportunity to increase their sales and beat the competition.

In 1975 manufacturers distributed approximately 35 billion cashoff coupons. In 1980 this figure will be pushing 90 billion. By 1981 it should easily top 100 BILLION!

"Who pay for cashoff coupons?"

Indirectly we all pay for manufacturers' advertising and promotion, and this includes the cost of cashoff coupons. The important question that each shopper should ask is "How much can I save with coupons?" If you organize your coupons the way I do, and use them effectively, you will be way ahead of the game. If you don't take advantage of coupon discounts, you have only yourself to blame.

Why Do Stores Redeem Cashoff Coupons?

The supermarkets know that cashoff coupons help to sell merchandise. So, it is in their best interest to cooperate with manufacturers who aggressively promote their products with coupons.

But the stores also have another reason for redeeming cashoff coupons. The manufacturers pay them a 5¢ handling fee for each coupon they redeem. This may not sound like much, but it is more profit than they make on a lot of items, and since they handle so many coupons each year, this amount really adds up.

Because stores make money on every coupon you turn in, they want your coupon business and they are happy to get it.

Double Value Coupons!

"Double Coupons"—two words that are a delight to any couponer.

When a store offers to double the value of manufacturers' cashoff coupons, shoppers with a large collection of coupons really cash in for big savings: A 10¢-off coupon is now worth 20¢, and a 50¢ coffee coupon saves you $1! Savings like these make it well worth traveling a few extra miles to find a store offering double coupons.

Why does a supermarket make this offer? Because it believes that this is an excellent way to bring in new customers—and it is! The lure of double savings is usually enough to bring in customers who shop at other stores. And hopefully these new customers will like the store and come back again.

When one store in a community offers double value coupons, it often leads to other stores doing the same. Eventually the stores get tired of this promotion and they end it. It is a costly promotion since they are paying for one-half of the shopper's double discount. But while double coupon savings are offered, the avid coupon clipper has a field day. It pays to stock up on often used items when a supermarket is making your 15 percent coupon discount into a 30 percent savings.

If stores in your area advertise double value coupons be sure to read their advertisements very carefully. Note that there may be restrictions and limitations. These generally apply to coffee and cigarettes. Some stores place a limit on the value of a coupon that can be doubled. Other stores may limit the number of coupons you can double on each shopping trip. Usually coupons for free products can't be doubled.

The Pride of a Couponer

When I walk up to the cashier with my purchases and hand her a thick wad of coupons, it is a moment of real pleasure. I have worked hard and used all of my skill to get these discounts, and I'm proud of every coupon I hand her. If she is efficient, it will only take her a few seconds more to total up my coupon savings.

As the cashier totals up my purchases and my savings I usually hear the reaction of the people in line behind me:

"How much did he save?"
"Twenty dollars! Thirty dollars!"
"How does he do it?"
"I wish I knew how to do that."

Yes, I'm really proud of being a couponer, and every couponer should take great pride in the money that is saved. Don't ever be embarrassed to redeem your cashoff coupons!

Remember, manufacturers are spending millions of dollars to get you to use coupons and buy their product. They want you to cash in on cashoff coupons.

Manufacturers aren't embarrassed to take your money, and you shouldn't feel the least bit embarrassed to take theirs!

FOUR COUPON DON'TS

- Don't hand the cashier a coupon that has expired.
- Don't hand the cashier a coupon for a product you haven't purchased.
- Don't hand the cashier a coupon good on a forty-eight-ounce size when you have selected a smaller size.
- Don't hand the cashier any kind of photocopy or counterfeit coupon.

Coupons, Coupons, Coupons

Manufacturers' cashoff coupons come in all sizes, styles and values. But, they share one common characteristic: Somewhere on the face of the coupon you will find the words "Store Coupon." This indicates that the shopper is to use them at the store as opposed to a refund form which is redeemed by mail.

Not many years ago the most common cashoff coupon had a value of 5¢. But with food prices going up, manufacturers have had to increase the value of their coupons in order to keep pace with inflation. Today the coupons that you will find most often have a value of 10, 15 or 25¢.

Most coupons have an expiration date that is several months after the date on which the coupon is distributed. Some coupons have no expiration date. Theoretically, they will be good for as long as the product is manufactured.

Some coupons contain a package-size requirement and are only good when that size is purchased.

Cashoff coupons contain language that is directed at the retailer such as "This coupon may not be assigned or transferred." This tells the store that it must

submit the coupon directly to the manufacturer or its agent, and can't sell or assign the the coupon to a third party. It is not a restriction on consumer couponers who want to trade, sell or otherwise legally dispose of their coupons.

Cashoff coupons usually contain language which indicates that the shopper must pay any applicable taxes. Therefore, if a product costs $1 and there is a 5 percent sales tax, the shopper must pay the full 5¢ tax even though they used a 25¢-off coupon which brought their actual cost down to 75¢. Since the store is being reimbursed the 25¢ by the manufacturer, it will have **actually** received the full dollar, all of which is taxable. But, if the store is offering double value coupons and the shopper doubles her 25¢-off coupon, the store should charge the tax based on a purchase price of 75¢.

Most coupons contain the words "Cash Redemption Value 1/20 of 1¢." These words are placed on the coupon because some states require that all coupons have some redemption value. Since cashoff coupons usually have a far greater value for the purpose of a purchase discount, I am not aware of instances where cashoff coupons were turned in for their cash redemption value.

Free Product Coupons

Manufacturers are increasingly using store coupons to give away samples of new products. Last year a well-known manufacturer of pet food distributed many millions of coupons offering a free 18-ounce box of the company's new cat food. Fortunately, not everyone has a cat and I haven't had to buy food for our cat Tiger even since!

Buy One—Get One Free Coupons

We also include in the category of cashoff coupons, those which offer the shopper an immediate product if they purchase one at the regular price. These coupons are real money savers because they give an immediate 50 percent discount.

Self-Destruct Coupons

A manufacturer making a coupon offer may want to give the shopper a choice of two sizes, or he may wish to make the coupon worth more if two packages are purchased rather than one. This can be accomplished in newspaper and magazine ads with a self-destruct type coupon. This is really two coupons in one, but in order to use one of them, the shopper must destroy the other.

"Use Now" and "Save Now" Coupons

A cashoff coupon that is being seen more often is the "Use Now" coupon. This is a coupon that the manufacturer attaches to the side of the box or package. The shopper pulls the coupon off the package at the checkout counter and immediately gets the discount.

Make Your Own Cashoff Coupon with a "Cash-in"

The latest innovation in cashoff coupons is the "Cash-in." A manufacturer with many products can use a cash-in coupon that allows the shopper to make cashoff coupons for the product needed.

On to one cashoff coupon the shopper can attach any one of several stick-ons indicating the product and the value of the coupon.

Some cash-in coupons allow the shopper to select several products and attach several stick-ons to get discounts on all of them.

Shoppers can expect to see a greater number of cash-in coupons in 1980. They will become more important as shoppers become familiar with them.

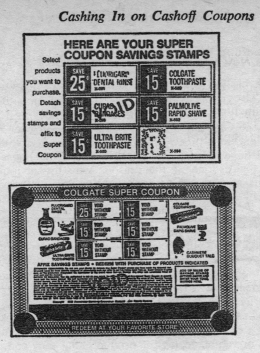

The "Signature" Coupon

To combat coupon fraud, some manufacturers are experimenting with cashoff coupons that require the shopper to fill in both name and address on the coupon. This helps to assure manufacturers that each coupon has been turned in by an actual purchaser of their products. Filling in a name and address takes only a few seconds, and it is a small price to pay for a money-saving discount.

Expanding Your Coupon Inventory

Most coupon clippers who get their cashoffs organized, and who start to use them consistently, wish that they had more of the coupons they need most. They clip out a coupon for apple juice or frozen french fries and wish that they had a dozen of each of them.

I have as many as 2,000 coupons to choose from and that is one of the reasons why my coupon discounts add up to big savings. You too can have this kind of coupon inventory if you follow these tips:

• Recruit your children and their friends to find coupons. If you offer them a penny for each good coupon, you will be amazed at their resourcefulness.
• Ask your non-couponing neighbors to save you the food section from their newspaper. I know a couponer who regularly gets more than a dozen papers this way.
• Ask your relatives to save you the coupons they don't need. (Be sure to occasionally give them coupons or refund forms for products that they can use.)
• If your paper is delivered to your door, ask the carrier for any food-day editions he may have left over.
• If you live in an apartment make friends with the fellow who handles the trash. Think of all the food sections and coupons he throws out each week!
• Check out the local recycling center. Old newspapers and magazines often have cashoff coupons that have not expired. You will be surprised at the coupon bonanza you find.

A Tip from *The Shopper:*

A super-smart shopper knows when to take advantage of a good thing. When the food section of a newspaper contains several dollars' worth of coupons, the easiest way to build up your coupon inventory is to buy a few copies.

More Tips from *The Shopper*:

Start a coupon exchange where you live, or where you work:

• If you live in an apartment, put a can or box or other container in the laundry room and mark it in large letters "COUPON EXCHANGE." Put a dozen cashoff coupons in the container and it is off to a good start. The next time you come down to do your laundry you will probably be surprised at all the coupons you find.

• Coupon clippers in rural areas who have a group of mailboxes can put a coupon exchange container nearby and make an exchange every time they go for the mail.

• At work you should get permission to put a coupon exchange container in your lunchroom or lounge. It's a great way to liven up your coffee breaks.

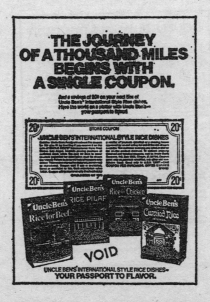

7

Double Play Discounts

One of the important secrets of using coupons and refunds is combining both discounts on the same product!

Most shoppers never realize that they could combine coupon and refund discounts on a substantial number of the products they use every day. Since they don't organize their coupons, and most of them don't know about refunds, they aren't in a position to spot these Double Plays. But, if you follow our couponing and refunding system, you should be able to find more than a dozen Double Plays each week. An example of a typical coupon and refund Double Play is seen on page 76.

"How much can I save by making a Double Play?"

Most Double Play discounts that combine a coupon and a refund save you 40 to 65 percent! Here is the simple addition that shows you why:

Your average discount from a cashoff coupon is 15 percent; add to this a refund of 25 to 50 percent and you have Double Play savings of 40 to 65 percent.

"Are Double Plays really available for a large number of supermarket products?"

Yes, many manufacturers distribute a steady stream of coupon and refund offers, and they are often made for the same product at the same time. One well-known coffee always seems to have several different cashoff coupons and a variety of interesting refund offers available. It is a challenge to the supersmart shopper to find these Double Play opportunities.

Each month *The National Supermarket Shopper* publishes a listing of Double Play discounts. The sample listing that appeared in last November's issue is shown below. A representative sampling of Double Play opportunities, and it was used to show A.C.C. members that combined discounts are readily available in almost every product category. Look for your own current Double Play discounts.

File #	Manufacturer/Product	Cashoff Coupon	Refund Offer
1	Beech-Nut Cera-Meal	25 cents	$1
1	Beech-Nut Fruits	15 cents	$1

File #	Manufacturer/Product	Cashoff Coupon	Refund Offer
1	Shedd's Spread	10 cents	Free Pkg.
1	Chex Cereals	25 cents	Snack Set
1	3-Minute Brand Oats	25 cents	$1
1	Wheaties	20 cents	Olympic Guide
2	Kaukauna Cheese Log	15 cents	$1
2	Slender Diet Bars	15 cents	50¢
2	Sunlite Oil	20 cents	$2
2	Land O Lakes Margarine	15 cents	$1
3	La Pizzeria	25 cents	$1
3	Chunky Candy Bar	12 cents	Jade Necklace
3	Chunky Candy Bar	12 cents	$1
3	Borden Singly Wrapped Slices	15 cents	50¢
3	Switzer's Candies	10 cents	$1
4	Birds Eye American Vegs.	10 cents	50¢
4	Hanover Salads	15 cents	50¢
4	Success Rice	50 cents	$1
5	Golden Griddle Syrup	10 cents	$1
5	Aunt Millie's Spag. Sauce	10 cents	50¢
5	Kraft Mayonnaise	10 cents	$1
5	Wish-Bone Dressings	15 cents	Free Btl.
5	Wish-Bone Creamy Italian	10 cents	Lettuce Refund
5	Wish-Bone Creamy Cucumber	15 cents	50¢
6	Certi-Fresh Fish Sticks	15 cents	$1
6	Van de Kamps Fish	35 cents	$1
6	Carnation Tuna	7 cents	$1
6	Oscar Mayer Breakfast Strips	20 cents	$1
6	Armour Vienna Sausage	15 cents	$1
6	Wilson Western Style Meats	40 cents	Poncho
7	Quick Bread	25 cents	Free Pkg.
7	Keebler Chocolate Chip	10 cents	Free Pkg.
7	Keebler Dougle Nutty/ Elfwich	10 cents	Free Pkg.
7	Betty Crocker Products	10–40 cents	$2
8	Hawaiian Punch	12 cents	75¢–$3.80
8	Nescafe Instant Coffee	50 cents	World Mug
8	Kool-Aid	25 cents	$1.20
8	Lemon Tree	40 cents	$1 Cpn.
8	Sanka	40 cents	$1 Cpn.
8	Mellow Toast	35 cents	$1

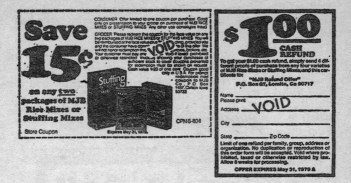

Although you will have to search for most coupon and refund Double Plays, manufacturers occasionally put both a coupon and a refund form in one advertisement and hand you a Double Play on a silver platter.

"When I combine a supermarket special with a coupon, is that a Double Play too?"

The term Double Play can describe any type of double discount. It can apply equally well to a supermarket discount combined with either a cashoff coupon or a refund. It can also apply to double coupon savings. As you will see in the Prestone illustration, some stores even advertise their Double Plays!

8

Supermarket Specials

Supermarket specials offer every couponer and refunder a tremendous opportunity to add to their supermarket savings. Most supermarkets and larger grocery stores offer specially priced items on a regular basis. These sale prices are usually advertised in the food section of the newspaper and smart shoppers may have several days in which to take advantage of them.

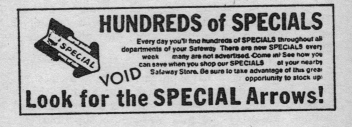

"How much can I save if I buy supermarket specials?"

Shoppers can save 15 to 25 percent by purchasing supermarket specials. Many supermarkets give up most or all of their profit in order to make their sale prices attractive.

Couponers and refunders find specials of great interest because they provide big discounts for products such as meat, dairy products, and produce for which there are few coupons and refunds.

Since you probably don't use an electronic calculator when you consider the savings you can obtain from supermarket specials, we have done some typical calculations for you:

Meat Purchase	Reg. Price Monday	Sale Price 3 days later	Savings per lb.	Percent Savings
Bottom Round Roast	$2.45	$1.89	$ .56	23%
Sirloin Steak	3.01	1.99	1.02	34%
Center-cut Pork Chops	2.11	1.49	.62	29%
Bacon	1.49	.99	.50	34%

"Why do the stores offer specials?"

A supermarket advertises sale priced specials in order to bring in new customers and keep those that it already has. Supermarket managers hope that customers will pick up a few specials and then purchase the rest of their needs at regular prices.

Many supermarket specials are the result of "deals" that store managers have purchased from their suppliers. The store purchases the deal at a lower-than-usual price and then passes along its savings to the shopper. Many of the new warehouse supermarkets concentrate on purchasing deals.

Store managers are very sensitive to the specials offered by their competition. If a nearby store offers Whole Fryers at 49¢ a pound, a store manager will try to come up with a special that is equally as good. This type of competition offers smart shoppers tremendous savings opportunities.

You Must Shop at Several Stores!

There is only one way to save money with supermarket specials. You must pick your specials from at least two or more stores!

It is a fact that you will save little or nothing if you only shop at one store. Why? Because stores that offer sale-priced specials must build additional profits into the prices of their other merchandise in order to stay in business. What you save by buying the specials at one store, you lose by making the rest of your purchases at regular prices.

If you would like proof that shopping for specials at only one store gets you nowhere, here it is:

A recent survey of ten supermarkets, all located in a major metropolitan area found the following:

• Prices for the same cut of beef varied by as much as 69 percent; the highest price of $2.69 was at a store where the meat was not on sale, and the lowest price of $1.59 was a supermarket special.

• Prices for produce varied by as much as 158 percent; the highest price for cabbage was 49¢ a pound in a store where it was not on sale, and the lowest price was a 19¢ special.

• Despite these substantial differences in prices, when a typical market basket of similar items was added up at each of the ten supermarkets, the differences between the store with the lowest total price and the store with the highest total price was less than 3 percent! The lowest total was $142.56 while the highest was $146.49.

Why did the lowest and highest market totals vary so much less than the prices of individual items? It seems obvious that these stores priced some items very competitively but made up the difference on the rest of their merchandise.

What would the cost of the total market basket be if a shopper had shopped at three or more of the stores selecting the best specials at each? We don't have an accurate figure because the research was not conducted in this way, but our best estimate is a savings of *more than 20 percent!*

Let Your Fingers Do The Walking . . .

The best and easiest way to shop for supermarket specials is to pick them out of the food section of your daily newspaper. At least once a week, usually Wednesday or Thursday, most newspapers carry a food section with numerous supermarket ads.

Look at the supermarket advertisements as one huge discount supermarket. In this very special "store" your objective is to find everything on your shopping list!

Pick up a pen or pencil—try a red one or any other color that will stand out—and let your fingers do the walking through the supermarket ads. Start with at least three supermarkets and select meat, poultry, fish, and other main dishes. If you shop once a week, try to pick out seven of the best and most interesting of these main dish specials.

The first time that you pick a week's worth of main dish specials you will have already saved more than $10. Yes, if you have selected seven dinners using supermarket specials, you will have saved more than $10! And, you have done it without substituting noodles for meat or cutting down on the size of the portions you serve.

Now that you have the main dishes selected, start looking for your side dishes. Perhaps one of the supermarkets is advertising a sale on fresh vegetables that would go well with the first few of your dinner selections. Another store may be featuring canned or frozen vegetables that you can use later in the week.

Continue to pick out money-saving specials for desserts, beverages, lunch and breakfast products. Before you let your fingers stop their walking, pick out the miscellaneous items such as cleaning products, pet food, and other items still left on your shopping list.

"Doesn't this limit my selections?"

If you live in a small town or have only one supermarket within easy traveling distance, the supermarket specials that are available to you will be limited. But, if you live in an area where there is a choice of several competitive supermarkets, all within a few minutes' drive, you probably have many hundreds of sale-priced specials to choose from each week. The average full-page supermarket advertisement contains from 50 to 100 sale-priced specials. Many daily newspapers have almost a dozen pages of supermarket ads, and there are often more than a thousand advertised specials.

When you fully realize the tremendous amount you can save by concentrating on supermarket specials, the chances are that you won't feel limited, especially if you are willing to be flexible and try new products and brands.

Restrictions

Most supermarket newspaper advertisements contain restrictions on sale-priced specials. The most common of these is a notice that the sale prices advertised will be effective for a specific period of time. You will find a notice such as this: *"Prices effective thru Saturday, June 24th."*

Stores frequently include language in their advertisements which gives them the right to limit the quantity of sale-price items each shopper can purchase: *"We reserve the right to limit sales to three packages of any sale item."* This doesn't mean that you can't pick up six packages of a sale item and take them to the checkout counter. The chances are that you would have no problem in purchasing them. But, if the supermarket runs low on a sale-priced item, *it may if it wishes* limit you to three packages. Similarly, some ads state that "sale items are not available in case lots."

Supermarket Coupons

Many supermarkets give attention getting impact to their sale-priced specials by advertising them in the form of coupons. In order to take advantage of these specials, shoppers must clip these coupons out and turn them in at the checkout counter in the same way they do with manufacturers' cashoff coupons.

Because of space limitations in supermarket advertisements, most supermarket coupons are smaller than manufacturers' coupons. They also don't have the legal language and redemption instructions found on a manufacturers' cashoff coupon. Supermarket coupons use the word "coupon," but not the words "store coupon" found on manufacturers' cashoffs.

One of the secrets of successful couponing is that you can usually use a supermarket coupon with a manufacturer's coupon for a double discount on the same item!

"Do the words 'one coupon per person' prevent me from combining a supermarket coupon and a manufacturer's coupon?"

No. This language usually means that you can't take two or more *supermarket coupons* and combine them on the same item. If a supermarket offers its own discount, this shouldn't conflict with the discount of a manufacturer's cashoff coupon.

It is important to be able to tell the difference between a supermarket coupon and a manufacturer's coupon that you may also find published in a supermarket newspaper advertisement. Supermarkets occasionally cooperate with manufacturers and print coupons in their supermarket advertisements which are actually manufacturers' cashoff coupons. These cashoffs may look like supermarket coupons, but somewhere on the coupon you will find words or abbreviations indicating that they are manufacturers' cashoff coupons.

The coupon above is a manufacturer's coupon that was published in a supermarket advertisement. It *can't* be used in combination with a regular manufacturer's cashoff coupon.

Rain Checks

Most supermarkets stock up on their advertised specials so that they have enough for all the customers who want them. But occasionally shoppers find that a sale item is out of stock.

What should you do when you arrive at the store expecting to purchase the 99¢ half-gallon of ice cream and find that it is out of stock?

Ask for a rain check, of course!

Unless the supermarket advertisement clearly indicates that there is a limited quantity of a specific sale item, you have a right to purchase it at the advertised price. After all, the supermarket has advertised the sale price to induce you to come into the store, and you should be able to make your purchase at that price. Therefore, if an advertised item does run out of stock, you have a right to receive a rain check which will allow you to purchase that product at the sale price at a future date.

Most stores willingly give their customers rain checks when they run out of an advertised special. They know that it is good customer relations to do so.

You will often see a notice in supermarket newspaper advertisements informing shoppers of this policy.

Rain checks are not all alike. The rights you receive can differ substantially. Some rain checks such as the one below from Gristede's are only good for a limited period of time, in this case one week. If the sale item is still not in stock at the end of the week, the shopper may be further inconvenienced.

A better rain check gives you thirty days in which to purchase the sale item. Some thoughtful supermarkets allow the shopper to substitute a comparable item for a sale item that is out of stock. And there are a few smart chains that really go out of their way to show their concern for customers who have been inconvenienced by items that are out of stock. The Shopwell "Bonus" rain check is a good example of this.

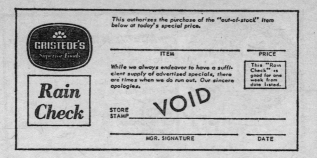

You should never be embarrassed to ask for a rain check. It shows that you are a smart shopper who knows what is rightfully yours. Walk right up to the manager's desk or the customer service desk and say "I'd like a rain check please."

9
_____

Triple Play!

The highest achievement for every super-smart shopper is a Triple Play discount. The most common Triple Play combines the discounts from a sale-priced supermarket special, a manufacturer's cashoff coupon, and a refund offer. A Triple Play can save you 70, 80, even 90 percent and more!

"How do I find a Triple Play?"

You have to become experienced at our game of match. You must sharpen your skill at remembering your coupons and refund forms and the many specials that crowd the supermarket ads. Each week as you put together the discounts for your shopping list and search for Double Plays, you will also come across Triple Play opportunities. It is bound to happen.

When you find your first Triple Play it is a real thrill.

Each month _The National Supermarket Shopper_ publishes an illustrated example of a Triple Play. The purpose is to show each A.C.C. member how simple it is to obtain tremendous discounts on supermarket products they use every day. The illustration shows a portion of a supermarket newspaper advertisement as discount number one; a cashoff coupon as discount number two; and a refund form which provides the third discount. At the bottom of the illustration is a savings summary which shows how much you can save when you combine these three discount opportunities. Here are examples of these Triple Play illustrations straight from the pages of *The National Supermarket Shopper :*

Free Food!

Yes, there are even Triple Play discounts that give you free food. Here are examples:

10

Keeping Score

Those persons who are employed have always been able to judge their achievements by the profits they make for their companies, and the money they earn for themselves. But, there has never been a really good monetary yardstick for supermarket shoppers to judge their own effectiveness or worth. In the past, supermarket savings of a few dollars a week were hardly noticed. Most shoppers find it difficult to save even that much today.

But couponing and refunding has brought something new to supermarket shopping: a skill that can be measured in big savings. Experienced couponers and refunders are able to save $20, $25, even $30 a week! These are very meaningful savings that can be put into the bank or provide a family with special things they otherwise might not have.

This ability to save substantial amounts of money is bringing to couponers and refunders a new and well-deserved recognition. They are receiving new respect at the dinner table and on the shopping line, and a lot of publicity in newspapers, on radio and television. It is only right that those who put so much time and energy into planning their shopping and their savings should be recognized for a job well done!

It's Fun To Keep Score

One of the most enjoyable parts of coupon clipping and super-smart shopping is keeping score of your savings.

It is fun to see your savings build up. At first, most of your savings will come from supermarket specials since you only need a newspaper to get started. But soon, as your inventory of coupons grows, so too will your savings. Finally, as the refunds start to roll in, you will see these combined savings turn into the $20, $25, and $30 a week that we have been talking about.

"How should I keep track of my savings?"

The best way to keep track of your savings is to use a scoreboard similar to that shown on the next page. It has spaces to record all of your savings from supermarket specials, coupons, and refunds. There is also space to record your expenses for envelopes and postage.

It is easy to keep track of your refund savings. Just write them down as they arrive in your mailbox. When you receive coupons for free products or gifts, estimate their value and put these amounts on your scoreboard too.

Sometimes your cashoff coupon savings will be totaled at the bottom of your cash register tape and in some cases they won't. In either case, be sure to circle them or write them down on the bottom of the tape. When you get home, remember to transfer this figure to your scoreboard.

The hardest savings to keep track of are those you receive from supermarket specials. The easiest way for most shoppers to keep track of these savings is to estimate them and jot down these estimates next to each special on your shopping list or Purchase Planner. If you save 30¢ on a box of detergent, just jot it down next to the item on your list. It is a little harder when your savings are by the pound. For instance, if you know that you are saving 23¢ a pound on a whole fryer and it weighs 4.25 pounds, you might as well estimate that your savings will be $1. It isn't exact, but it is as accurate as you need to be in order to keep track of your savings.

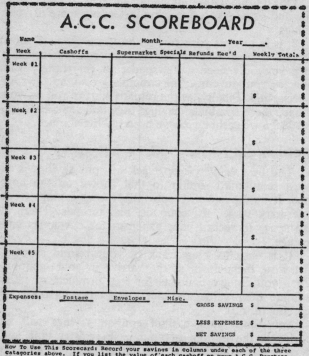

A.C.C. SCOREBOARD

Week	Cashoffs	Supermarket Specials	Refunds Rec'd	Weekly Totals
Week #1				$
Week #2				$
Week #3				$
Week #4				$
Week #5				$

Name_____ Month_____ Year_____.

Expenses: Postage____ Envelopes____ Misc.____

GROSS SAVINGS $ _____
LESS EXPENSES $ _____
NET SAVINGS $ _____

How To Use This Scorecard: Record your savings in columns under each of the three categories above. If you list the value of each cashoff on your A.C.C. Purchase Planner, you can easily take the total off that sheet and transfer it to this score-card. It is often difficult to calculate your savings from supermarket specials, but make the best estimates that you can. Record refunds as they are received. Show the retail value of refund product bonuses. List all expenses.
Copyright 1978 American Coupon Club, Inc.

"What do most coupon clippers do with the money they save?"

Most couponers and refunders actually take the money they receive from cashoff coupons and refund offers and they save it. Many of them save up for a family vacation. Disney World seems to be the most popular choice. Some put these monies into special savings accounts for their children.

In these times of rising food prices, it is very hard for anyone to save money. But the fact that coupon and refund cash comes back to you *after* you have already spent it, seems to make it a lot easier to put away in a savings account.

Tip from *The Shopper:*

Whenever you put your savings into a cookie jar or candy tin there is always a temptation to reach in and spend the money on a lot of little things. If your savings go out just as fast as they come in, they won't mean very much to you. If you let your savings build up, you really feel like you are accomplishing something wonderful. This is especially true when the whole family is saving for an important goal.

In order to control their desire to reach into the cookie jar, most smart coupon clippers figure out a way to discourage themselves from doing this. One refunder I know converts all her coupon savings into quarters and puts them into rolls. As soon as she has a full roll, she seals it very carefully. She would never dream of opening one of these rolls. Many smart refunders make it a practice to deposit their savings in the bank whenever they add up to $5. They happily watch the numbers in their savings account pass book grow.

11

Your Shopping List

You can clip hundreds of coupons, find lots of refund forms, and save boxes of POP's, but it won't mean a thing unless you use a shopping list to organize and plan your savings. The shopping list brings all your discount opportunities together and puts them in a manageable form.

Can you get by without a list? Not really. Imagine going to several supermarkets without a shopping list and trying to remember which one had the celery on sale. Imagine trying to pick out your coupon items without a list. You would find yourself walking up and down the same aisles again and again.

With a shopping list you don't have to carry around the supermarket newspaper ads, and you can leave your refund forms safely at home.

First, Make Yourself an "I need" List

I need pancake mix
I need Swiss cheese
I need trash bags
I need light bulbs—60 watt

I need olives (with pits)
I need spaghetti—1 lb.
I need spaghetti sauce
I need ....

As you find that you need certain supermarket products, put them on an "I need" list. These are the items that you will buy on your next regular shopping trip. Try to avoid putting brand names on this list.

The Master Plan

Your shopping list is your master plan for victory at the supermarket.
You are the general.
Bring on the troops!

Step 1

List your main dish supermarket specials. You should try to plan for at least five of your dinners if you shop once a week. Next, list the rest of the specials that you have picked out of the newspapers, the ones you will use for lunches and breakfasts.

Next, work from your "I need" list to find specific advertised specials for the products you have listed.

Step 2

By this time you will have your supermarket specials on your shopping list and you will probably still have a few items left on the "I need" list for which you haven't found supermarket specials. Start Step 2 by looking through your inventory of cashoff coupons for the balance of these "I need" items.

Next, look at the supermarket specials on your shopping list and try to find cashoff coupons for each of them. As you look through your coupons you may find high value cashoffs, "buy one—get one free" offers and other special coupons that you want to take advantage of; add these items to your shopping list.

Step 3

Now is the time to work your refunds into this master plan. First, check your refund forms. Do you have any for the products you have already put on your shopping list?

Look for high value refunds and those for products you normally use, and try to work these refunds into your shopping list.

Next, check the refund offers listed in my newspaper column or the Clip'n File refund lists found in *The National Supermarket Shopper*. Even if you don't have these refund forms, you now know how to find them. So, if you find an interesting refund listing for a product you use or want to try, work the product into your shopping list if you can. By "working a product into the list" we mean that you should try to put it on the list if it has a useful place. If you find a good refund for frozen vegetables, but your shopping list has more than enough vegetable items already on it, then forget about the refund until next week.

Play "Match"

As you go through your coupons and refunds and look through the supermarket ads, play a game of "match." Try to match specials with your coupons, and try to match coupons with refunds and refunds with specials. This is the way to find your combined Double Play and Triple Play discounts.

The A.C.C. Purchase Planner

The American Coupon Club has developed a simple shopping list for couponers and refunders. It is called the "A.C.C. Purchase Planner" and it combines an "I need" list with a five-day shopping list that is divided into breakfasts, lunches and dinners.

Copyright 1979 American Coupon Club, Inc. A.C.C. PURCHASE PLANNER	Dates Used

	Day #1	Day #2	Day #3	Day #4	Day #5	"I need" List
Breakfast Products						
Lunch Products						
Dinner Products						
Misc. Food Products						
Non-Food Products					Notes	Savings
Codes	Supermarkets: ①_____ ②_____ ③_____				*=no coupon	

The A.C.C. Purchase Planner allows you to list three supermarkets at the bottom so you can use the circled one, two, and three codes next to the supermarket specials to show which stores are offering the specials. You will have cashoff coupons for most of the items on your Planner, but you should remember to put a star next to those for which you don't have a coupon. This will save you needless searching for a coupon that doesn't exist. In the box on the lower right you can make an estimate of your savings from supermarket specials.

"Why does the Planner only have room for five days' worth of purchases?"

The reason why the Planner isn't a Monday through Sunday shopping list is to emphasize that couponing and refunding doesn't have to be a seven-day-a-week effort in order to provide you with meaningful savings. The vast majority of couponers and refunders find that five days' worth of important savings is sufficient to meet their money-saving objectives. There are always recipes that you will want to try that offer no discount opportunities. There is also the dinner that you will want to eat out and treat your family and yourself to with some of your savings. If each week you make up a shopping list similar to the A.C.C. Purchase Planner, you should be very proud of yourself if you fill in all the boxes with money-saving specials, coupon and refund savings.

Planning Menus with Coupons and Refunds

Many experienced couponers and refunders find it a challenge to plan a full day's menu using all their discount opportunities. Here is an example:

Breakfast

Snow Crop Orange Juice—on sale, plus 10¢-off, plus $1 refund.

Aunt Jemima Jumbo Waffles—50¢ refund.

Golden Griddle Syrup—10¢-off, plus $1 refund.

Maxwell House Coffee—on sale, plus 40¢-off, plus offer of coupon wallet—and 90¢ in coupons.

Lunch

La Choy Beef Pepper Oriental Chow Mein—on sale, plus 15¢-off, plus offer of free can.

Tetley Instant Tea—50¢-off, plus $1.10 cookie money refund.

Dinner

Soup made with Soup Starter—on sale, 20¢-off, plus free package offer.

Hamburger Stroganoff—meat on sale.

Noodles—on sale, Pennsylvania Dutch Noodles $1 refund offer.

Ragù Spaghetti Sauce—on sale, plus free jar offer.

Vegetables from Seabrook Farms—50¢ refund.

Salad—Lettuce refund from Pfeifer, 15¢-off on Wish-Bone, plus free bottle offer.

Sara Lee Original Butter Recipe Cake—on sale, 10¢-off, plus $1 refund.

Shop Infrequently!

One of the secrets of super-smart shopping is to shop no more than once a week. Try to stretch it to once every ten days if you can. Pretend that you are going to spend the next week or ten days on a desert island so that you must buy *everything* you will need. When you are on a desert island you can't run out to the store in an emergency.

Why is this good advice? Think about it for a minute:

First, if you are purchasing for a week or more, chances are that you will make a quick check of the food that you presently have on hand. This results in less waste and duplication.

Second, if you will be on a desert island without a handy 7-11 around the corner, the chances are you will be more careful and complete in your planning. It is less likely that you will forget Jell-O or the salad dressing. Every time you are forced to "run out to the store" you are purchasing without the good planning and without the discounts that save you the most money.

12

The Shopping Safari

Supermarket shopping should be fun! With more than 1,000 products to choose from, it should be an adventure.

It is for me because when I leave for the stores, the hard work is already done. The clipping, the filing, the circling, the planning, and the writing are already

behind me. I have my shopping list in my pocket, and it is full of supermarket specials, coupon discount items, and products I need to get cash and free product refunds.

When I go shopping I already know that I'm getting a discount on almost every item on my shopping list. On many of them, I will be getting Double Play and Triple Play discounts! This certainly does a lot for my sunny disposition. It is great to look at a long shopping list that you know should add up to about $100 and realize that after the discounts it will cost just about $50!

It is easy to understand why I walk into the supermarket smiling and full of energy. For me, shopping is a safari, an adventure where I hunt for unexpected bargains.

So, stop moaning about supermarket inflation. You too can make shopping a pleasure if you organize your coupons, get interested in refunds, and pay attention to supermarket specials. When you start to make those big Double Play and Triple Play discounts and get "coupon fever," you will look forward to every trip to the supermarket just as I do.

Entering the Hunting Grounds

Before you walk into the supermarket, be sure to check out the window posters. Most supermarkets advertise some of their sale-priced specials on these window posters. Occasionally they offer bargains that were not included in the store's newspaper advertisement. Be sure to check out store circulars that are found at the door. These circulars may have specials that the manager was not able to fit into the newspaper ad.

SMPs—Specially Marked Packages

A shopper's riddle: *After you have given your cashoff coupons to the cashier, how do you walk out of the supermarket with more coupons than you came in with?*

Answer: *By purchasing specially marked packages which have cashoff coupons printed on their backs or tucked inside.*

I return from every shopping safari with a bonus of cashoff coupons and refund forms that I find on specially marked packages. Many shoppers hardly notice these specially marked packages with their bright banners and bursts of color proclaiming the special offers that are to be found inside or on the back of the package. But once you start looking for them, you will find them on almost every shelf.

"Is it really worth the trouble to look for SMPs?"

YES, it certainly is. More manufacturers are waking up to the sales appeal of high value SMP offers. It is not unusual to find several cashoff coupons on the back of a package with a total value almost equaling the price of the package itself. I recently paid 79¢ for a box of Rice Chex and the cashoff coupons on the back were worth 71¢! And these were not just cereal coupons. They included discounts on Libby's canned fruit, Sweet'N Low, Downyflake Waffles, Golden Griddle Syrup, Welch's jellies, and Borden Instant Breakfast Drink.

You will also find SMPs with refund forms. In some supermarkets there are more forms on the SMPs than on pads attached to the shelves.

Tip from *The Shopper:*

Experienced couponers pick a package off the supermarket shelf and if it isn't an SMP they always take a quick look at the other packages, especially those at the back, to see if an SMP is left over from a previous shipment. You will be surprised at how often this happens and you are able to walk away with the bonus of an SMP. Once in a while this quick look will also reveal a few packages that are marked with lower prices!

Hunting for Refund Forms

As I work my way down the aisles, I'm looking at every shelf for refund forms.

If you have to shop with children, you can put the older ones to work searching for refund forms.

When I find a pad of refund forms I follow the "A.C.C. Rules of Fair Play" and take only *two*, one for my own use and one to trade.

Searching for Bargains

Finding unexpected bargains is one of the joys of supermarket shopping.

Occasionally a shipment arrives after the store's newspaper ad has been finalized or the manager finds that he suddenly has too much of an item. In these cases, store managers react quickly with a special display and some hand-painted "Sale" signs.

You will often find these unadvertised specials stacked at the end of the aisles, or even in the aisles so that you are sure to notice them.

> **Warning:** Just because an item is stacked at the end of an aisle and has a big price sign above it doesn't mean that it is a bargain. Some stores create these end-of-aisle displays with regular price merchandise because they know that this position attracts special customer attention. It pays to check the prices to know whether or not you are really getting a bargain.

Become Friendly with the Natives

Many shoppers look for the supermarket manager

only when they want to complain about something. This is a great mistake!

Every super-smart shopper knows that having a store manager as a friend will save many dollars at the checkout counter. Here are just a few of the ways that the manager can help you:

- He can give you refund forms that are left with him by manufacturers' salesmen.
- He can tell you about sales that are coming up so that you can plan to take advantage of them.
- He can help you get discounts on cans with missing labels. He is the expert and usually knows what's inside them!
- He will tell you where and when you can find day-old bread, reduced-price produce, and other special bargains.
- He can give you advice that will help you make better selections, such as telling you the store's schedule for putting out fresh meat and produce.
- He can help you to read the product-dating codes so you can be sure that the food you are buying has been freshly packaged.
- If there is a mailing list that the store uses to send out special notices, coupons and such, he can put your name on it.
- Having the manager as a friend makes it a lot easier to ask for a rain check or return bad merchandise.
- He can introduce you to other refunders, or help you put up a sign announcing your coupon swap session or your new coupon club.

What can you do for the manager in return?

First, if you enjoy shopping at his store, tell him so.

A compliment is always a good way to start a friendship.

Have you seen a few of his shopping carts behind the fence at the Little League field? Store managers appreciate being told where their expensive carts have disappeared to.

I recently found a six-pack of soda in one of the

store's open freezer chests. Someone had thoughtlessly dropped it there. My friend the manager was happy to learn of it before the bottles broke and ruined other merchandise. There are lots of ways to show your appreciation if you look for them.

Comparing Prices

Even though you have spent a lot of time preparing a shopping list full of money saving items, you should never feel bound by your list. If you spot a better bargain, you should buy it. This means that when you are about to pick up an item that is on your shopping list, you should first look up, down, left and right in order to check out the competition. It doesn't make much sense to use a 7¢-off coupon on an 89¢ item when a competing brand equally as good is priced at 79¢.

You should also check to see whether the larger size is a better bargain. It used to be that larger sizes were always the better buy, but not so today. Check the unit prices and you will see that the larger sizes of some products offer little price advantage.

Comparing prices can be difficult if the competing brands have different package sizes. It often seems that manufacturers use a 15-ounce size box just to make it harder to figure out the price per pound, and competing brands use different sizes so that it will be harder to compare their prices. In order to help shoppers make meaningful comparisons, several states have enacted unit price laws which require that food stores show a unit price in addition to the price of the item. This means that the supermarket and the manufacturers do all the calculations for you, so you can compare the price of various brands even though they come in different sizes.

What can you learn from unit prices? A lot of interesting things: On a recent trip to the supermarket I took a careful look at the unit prices of dry cereals. 77¢ didn't seem like a lot for a six-pack of assorted individual servings of cereal, but when I looked at the unit price it was $2.46 per pound! I checked this against the large size of my favorite corn flakes, with a unit price of only 69¢ a pound—what a difference! I decided that I wasn't willing to pay almost $2 a pound more for the convenience of single servings.

On this same trip I decided to check the price of sugar-coated cereals, the ones that my children had eaten so much of when they were small. I looked at the most popular brand and found that the unit price was $1.48 a pound. The difference between one pound of the sugar-coated cereal and my corn flakes could almost pay for a five-pound bag of sugar!

Many shoppers say that they would like to check unit prices, but they forget to do it when they are in the supermarket. I have found that the best way to get yourself into the habit of comparing prices is to start with an interesting product that comes in many varieties and sizes. Bread is an item that has many interesting price differences that will become obvious to you when you check unit prices. The price of enriched white bread can vary by as much as 100 percent depending on the size and brand you select. Once you benefit from checking unit prices you will want to do it again.

If the supermarkets in your area are not required to post unit prices, you can usually calculate the unit prices yourself by dividing the number of ounces into the cost of the product. This gives you a cost per ounce which you can then compare to the cost per ounce of other sizes or other brands.

Tip from *The Shopper:*

When you are shopping at several supermarkets for their sale-priced specials, it also pays to keep track of their prices on often-used items that may not be frequently discounted. Bread, eggs, soda, milk, and other dairy products are some of the items you should keep track of.

Make up a list of these items and others that your family uses frequently and keep a simple record of their prices at the various stores in which you shop. Saving a few pennies on each of them adds up. Then, when you see an advertisement for one of these items you will know whether or not it is a real bargain and whether or not you should stock up on it.

Generic "No Frills" Products

"Where do the no-frills products fit into a couponer's shopping list?"

Wherever they make money saving sense.

Generic no-frills products are the lower-in-cost products that are now being offered in plain packages with simple black and white labels.

These products were first offered by a supermarket chain as a special promotion to bring in new customers. The idea caught on and has been widely copied by most of the supermarket chains around the country.

The generic no-frills products have great appeal because they are usually priced at 25 to 30 percent less than national brands and 10 to 20 percent less than the supermarket's own brand.

Why do these no-frills products cost less?

They cost less because of the absence of the usual frills that come with branded products: They have no high-power advertising, no fancy packages, and no fancy labels. All of these frills increase the cost of branded merchandise.

The generic "no frills" products cost less because they are usually lower in quality than national and house brands. This doesn't mean that they are nutritionally inferior, only that they may be below the grading standards used by the national brands. For instance, a national brand of cut green beans will have a uniform color and size. The no-frills brand will have beans that vary in color and size. You will find short pieces and ends of the beans.

Shoppers who have learned to save money with generic no-frills products have usually experimented with many different varieties in order to find a few that they are pleased with. They have substituted them for national brands without telling their families in order to get an unbiased reaction. Because the price of no-frills soda is so much less than the national brands, they have conducted blind tastings for their children to see if they could taste the difference.

One thing that should be remembered: You can't make Double Play and Triple Play discounts with generic no-frills products. So, smart shoppers can usually save more money when they buy national brand products that offer coupon and refund discounts.

Bagging Your Trophies—Checking Out

The hunt is over. Now it is time to enjoy what you have accomplished.

Checking out at the cash register is one of the happiest moments for every couponer and refunder. This is a moment of glory when your hard work really pays off. At the cash register you see in very definite terms how good a shopper you really are. And if you are good, everyone around you will know it and admire you for it.

At the checkout counter you will be able to help the cashier if you do the following:

• Face all your purchases toward the cashier with the price label up.
• Place the items for which you have cashoff coupons at the front so it will be easier for the cashier to check them.
• Hand the cashier your cashoff coupons and your coupons for free products *before* she starts ringing up your purchases.
• Circle the expiration dates on your coupons so the cashier will be able to check them quickly.

Tip from *The Shopper*:

Don't forget to ask the cashier if she has any refund forms tucked under the counter. You'll be surprised at how often you find them this way.

A Successful Safari

If you walked into the supermarket with a smile on your face and a shopping list full of savings, you are certainly going to walk out of the store even happier:

- with a lot more money left in your pocket.
- with unadvertised bargains that saved you even more than you had expected,
- with packages that have the boxtops and labels you will soon turn into refund cash,
- with SMPs and refund forms that will provide you with future savings.

Isn't this the way that you would like to shop?

13

Supermarket Shopping 1980

This year, you will most likely see these changes and trends in supermarket shopping:

Food Prices Going Up!

Throughout the chain of food production, from farmer to supermarket, increases in the cost of labor, energy and transportation will have a direct impact on food prices. As food prices climb, beef will lead the way. You can expect $2 a pound hamburger by this summer. More shoppers will switch to pork and poultry and other beef substitutes. By the end of 1980 you can expect that food prices will have increased more than 15 percent!

More Warehouse and Limited Assortment Stores

The big news in shopping for 1980 is the warehouse and limited assortment store. These are the new "no frills" food stores that offer a limited variety of grocery products at rock-bottom prices.

118

These new stores typically carry from 600 to 2,000 products compared to the 10,000 found in the average supermarket. Some concentrate on their own house brands, some carry national brands, and others have a variety of labels. But they all try to give you prices that are 15 to 20 percent below those you would pay at the supermarket.

In order to give you these savings, warehouse and limited assortment stores don't carry fresh meats, dairy or frozen products, or only a limited number of them. They display their merchandise in cartons and ask you to bag your own purchases. They even charge you extra for the bags. Most don't accept checks.

Shopper response to warehouse and limited assortment stores has been excellent. Almost every supermarket chain will be starting or expanding its own warehouse store operations in 1980. If they are not already in your area, they're coming soon!

Generic "No Frills" Products Are Alive and Well

NO-NAME GENERICS MEAN VALUE, YOU'VE TRIED IT AND FOUND IT TRUE!

Like any new innovation, generic labeling of food and non-food products required a trial period to determine whether the quality and value claims were valid. Well, they've passed the test. With flying colors. Every day more and more Waldbaum customers are making the generic section their first in-store stop. With notable savings in their shopping costs.

We're delighted. And we promise to keep working toward broadening our No Name generic selection to include more super-value products for you.

VOID

In 1979 supermarkets considered generic no-frills products to be only a promotion to bring in new customers. The chains make less profit on these plain label products, and most supermarkets had planned to discontinue them by the summer of 1979. But many shoppers found no-frills products that both saved them money and pleased them, and the stores are afraid that they will lose customers if they are discontinued.

Competition from warehouse stores are giving no-frills products a further boost. Some supermarkets now see them as a way to fight this new competition.

Most supermarkets still display their generic no-frills products in a corner or other out-of-the-way place. But a few supermarkets that want to help customers make meaningful price comparisons, put their no frills on the same shelves with comparable national and house brands. One supermarket recently offered shoppers a tasting of their no-frills products.

Fewer Games And Gimmicks

You will see fewer games and gimmicks in supermarkets this year. Most shoppers realize that these

contests, bingo games, and sweepstakes just add to the prices they pay. Even if they play the games, they rarely come out ahead. Interest in trading stamps still continues to decline.

With food prices climbing sky-high, supermarket executives have gotten the message: Shoppers don't want costly games and gimmicks. What they do want is lower prices, more supermarket specials, and discount opportunities.

Computerized Cash Registers

By the beginning of this year, more than 1,200 supermarkets had converted to the use of computerized cash registers. By the end of 1980 this number is expected to more than double.

The computerized cash register uses an electronic scanning device to read the Universal Product Code on each product you purchase. The cashier passes the UPC symbol over the scanner, and the information contained within the thick-and-thin black lines is flashed to the store's computer. Almost instantly, the computer transmits the price of the item to the cash register and your purchase is rung up.

The computerized cash register is faster than a cashier checking price labels. Because of this you will find that lines at the checkout counter will move more quickly.

```
SERVICE IS OUR GOAL

   FOOD TOWN
   THANKS YOU
  L-F-P-I-N-C
STORE #54  0//25/78


JOURNAL          .95A
CAMELS          3.59A
PEACHES          .47E
PEPSI           1.05E
BT DEP           .60H
CAT FOOD         .17A
      16/1.00
MAC DNR          .76D
VNILLA EX        .74E
CAT FOOD         .17A
      16/1.00
SOUP             .23E
G GAR BAG       1.04A
BRO MIX          .75E
SPAG DINR        .95E
COMT RICE        .64E
TAXCOL           .43H

     TOTAL     12.54

     CASH      12.54

     CHANGE      .00

0230   1 3  6.18PM
```

Sample receipt

These new marvels of the computer age also provide shoppers with a more detailed receipt. Next to the price they can also print the brand name of the product. They also provide the stores with important inventory sales information in a fraction of the time it used to take. This allows the store to gauge its requirements more efficiently and cut down on waste.

But many shoppers feel that computerized cash registers also present a danger to both their pocketbooks and their sanity. They fear that supermarkets will discontinue putting price labels on individual products once they convert to these new devices. Some supermarket chains have indicated that they are considering such a move. The stores say that eliminating individual price markings will reduce their labor costs.

Shoppers are not enthusiastic about the idea of walking up to the cash register with a cart full of items with no price markings. How will they know whether the price rung up by the computer is the right price? Computers are only as good as the people who program the prices into them.

Eight states now protect their supermarket shoppers with laws that require individual price markings on food products. Consumer activists are now working to enact similar legislation in other states. This issue promises to be a heated one.

14

"Dear Supermarket Shopper"

Each day I receive hundreds of letters from supermarket shoppers all over the country who read my newspaper column. Many of them are new to couponing and refunding and need help getting started. Others, have a great deal of experience and want to share their knowledge.

Here are a few of these letters which I hope you will find interesting.

Letters to Supermarket Shopper

Getting Free Gifts

Dear Supermarket Shopper:

Here is a hint that your readers may want to think about. I send for all the manufacturers' offers of free toys, children's items and gifts, even though I have no children.

I use these things for Christmas and birthday gifts for little friends and relatives. If a friend is in the hospital, I also have something to take to them.

It is also nice to put these items in the com-

munity Christmas baskets. Our town gives out more than 150 baskets to needy families every year, and more than 300 children enjoy their Christmas a little more because of them. I try to encourage clubs and ladies groups to send for these gifts so there will be enough to fill every basket.

My husband and I are on a fixed income and don't have money for all the gifts we would like to give at Christmas time, but through refunding I have lots of gifts to give these needy children. Sincerely yours,

Shirley T.
Cleveland, OK

Dear Shirley:
You are an inspiration to all of us, and we send you our best and warmest holiday wishes.

Rejection Letters

Dear Supermarket Shopper:
After waiting several weeks for a $1 refund, I just received my proofs of purchase back with a rejection letter. The letter says that I didn't have the proper number of proofs. But I did staple the right number to a 3" × 5" card. If the person counting them had looked carefully, they would have seen this. Obviously they gave the card a quick look and didn't see that they were all there. Who should I complain to? Who will reimburse me for all the postage I have spent?

Lorraine T.
Pittsburgh, PA

Dear Lorraine:
The refund clearing houses used by manufacturers do make mistakes. The person who looked at your refund request, has to sort through many thousands of them each day. There is only a second or two to look at each of them, and sometimes this isn't enough.

You sent the proper proofs and your should certainly complain about the mistake. But, the complaint should be sent to the manufacturer's Customer Relations Department, and not to the clearing house. Experience has shown that you will get better results by going straight to the "horse's mouth." Ask the manufacturer to also refund your postage. Most manufacturers' customer relations departments are very considerate of customers with complaints such as yours. You can find the manufacturer's address on the product package. Even if there is just a city and a zip code, your letter will get there.

Saving Time and Money

Dear Supermarket Shopper:
I really need to save money and I would like to try, but I work and don't have a lot of free time for coupons and refunds. Are there any shortcuts that you can recommend?

Wendy J.
Philadelphia, PA

Dear Wendy:
Here is a shortcut for you and other readers who want to start saving at the supermarket but don't feel that they have enough time.
Basic couponing will only take you thirty minutes each week and can save you $20 an hour!

Just do these things:

1. *Clip every coupon you can find (15 minutes each week).*
2. *File all your coupons into easy-to-use product groups, the same ones that we use to list our refund offers (5 minutes each week).*
3. *Look through your coupon files and try to find a coupon for every item on your weekly shopping list (10 minutes).*

That's all there is to it. Once your inventory of coupons builds up, you will save as much as $10 on your weekly trip to the supermarket. $10 for 30 minutes of couponing works out to $20 an hour.

Family Refunding

Dear Supermarket Shopper:

I'm 15 years old and I started refunding with my mother a few months ago. We now have over $100 in a savings account for something the family may agree on in the future. I hope that it will be a stereo set for the den.

The whole family saves labels and other proofs of purchase and everyone searches for refund forms. But it is my job to file away the coupons and refund forms.

My father finds it hard to believe that I have gotten so interested in refunds. You should have seen the surprised look on his face one day when he jokingly asked whether I wanted him to save the Frito bag, and I said YES! He was even more surprised when I showed him the $1 refund form that asked for it.

I wish I could tell you how pleased I am now that I can read about coupons and refunds twice a week in your column.

Carole W.
Wheeling, IL

Dear Carole,

I am proud to have a refunder like yourself as a reader. Families that refund together definitely have more FUN!

Saving Postage

Dear Supermarket Shopper:

While sending off some refund requests I realized that many were going to the same place in El Paso, Texas. Is it possible to send more than

*one refund in an envelope with the specific post
office box noted on each refund? It would certainly
save on postage.*

Kay
Pittsburgh, PA

Dear Kay,
Even though all your refund requests to El
Paso, Texas zip code 79977 go to the same clearing house, it isn't a good idea to send several different refund requests in one envelope. Most clearing houses are set up to sort refund requests based
on the post office box number found on the outside
of the envelope. If your envelope has one P.O.
box number on the outside and several different
refund requests inside, there is a great risk of its
not being properly processed.
It is possible for several refunders to save postage by putting their separate refund requests for
the same refund in one envelope addressed to the
same post office box number.

Teens Saving Money

Dear Supermarket Shopper:
I have been couponing for 15 years. I've saved
many dollars through the years but my biggest
pleasure is when my teenage daughters ask if they
can check my coupon file before they go shopping.
Once a few months ago, they saw hair spray on
sale for 49¢ and they needed some. It was a good
buy at 49¢, but they decided to check my cashoff
coupons. They found seven 15¢-off coupons and
bought seven cans. The cashier complimented
them on the way they purchased their hair spray.
They were all smiles when they got home and
told us their shopping experience. The pride that
my husband and I feel can't be put into words.
There are so many good lessons that can be
learned from couponing and refunding. In our
home it has been a wonderful teaching tool.

Now that your column is in the newspaper we enjoy our supermarket shopping even more.

> Mary B. and daughters
> Katherine, Margaret, and Elizabeth
> Chicago, IL

Dear Mary,
　You have taught your daughters a lesson that will always benefit them. You and your husband certainly have a right to be proud.

Counterfeit Refund Forms

Dear Supermarket Shopper:
　I recently started trading refund forms by mail with a few friends in other cities. So far the results have been great and I have a lot of new forms. But, one of the forms I received looks suspicious. On the back of the form is printed a description of another manufacturer's refund offer. I think that it is some kind of a counterfeit. What should I do with it?

> S.N.
> Spokane, WA

Dear S.N.:
　It certainly sounds like a counterfeit. If it is, you shouldn't try to use it. When manufacturers spot counterfeit forms they usually throw away both the form and your proofs of purchase. If the manufacturer decides to take action against you, it could be a very embarrassing situation.
　When I receive a counterfeit or a photocopy of a refund form I send it back with a note saying that I won't trade with the sender again if I receive any more. It usually works and I advise all refunders to follow this procedure.

Requesting Refund Forms

Dear Supermarket Shopper:
　I have heard that it's possible to write to

*Procter & Gamble for several refund forms.
Is this correct and can you give me their address?*

L.C. Houston, TX

Dear L.C.:

Procter & Gamble will send you several different refund forms if you request them. They will even refund your postage and give you an extension slip if the refund offer is close to expiration. You can send your request on a postcard, but be sure to name the specific refund offers that you are interested in. Merely putting down the name of the product is not enough.

To request refund forms from P&G, write to: Box 432, Cincinnati, OH 45299.

A tip about P&G refunds: In most cases they will accept several smaller size proofs that equal the required larger size.

Double Plays

Dear Supermarket Shopper:

Can you really use a supermarket coupon and a manufacturer's cashoff coupon to get two discounts on the same item? I have always thought about trying it but never have.

*G. C.
Milwaukee, WI*

Dear G.C.:

YES! In most cases you can use the coupon that you find in a supermarket's newspaper ad in combination with a regular manufacturer's cashoff coupon. This is what we call a Double Play discount.

But there are two exceptions to this general rule. You should be sure to look at the supermarket coupon carefully. If you find "MFGR" or something similar on it, it is actually a manufacturer's coupon that the store has included in its ad as part of a cooperative advertising program. Although it may otherwise look like a supermarket coupon it can't be used in combination with a regular manufacturer's coupon.

Some supermarket coupons say "One coupon per item purchased." This usually means that the store won't let you use more than one of their own coupons for each item and you can make your double play discount. But, a few stores interpret this to mean that you can only use one coupon of any kind.

Cash Register Tapes

Dear Supermarket Shopper:
If two different refund offers ask for cash register tapes and I buy both products at the same store, can I send each of the manufacturers half of the tape?

C.M.
Los Angeles, CA

Dear C.M.:
Manufacturers who ask for a cash register tape as a proof of purchase usually want the whole tape. It is additional evidence that you purchased the product. One way to solve your problem is to ask the cashier to ring up your refund purchases separately. But be sure that you do this when the store isn't crowded and there is no one waiting in line behind you.

Here are some more tips on tapes:

Be sure to circle the purchase price of the refund product, even if the refund requirements don't specifically request you to do so.

Experienced refunders save all their cash register tapes so that they are never at a loss for a required tape.

Triple Play!

Dear Supermarket Shopper:

One of the markets in our area offered Jeno's
Pizza on special—"Buy One and Get One Free."
The cost of one pizza was $1.59 and with a 25¢-
off coupon I was able to get two for $1.34. But
I didn't stop with this double play discount. I had
a refund form that offered me a free Jeno's Pizza
for two proofs of purchase. So, I made a triple
play and got three pizzas for $1.34!

Being a new refunder I was really pleased
with myself and I want to thank you for all the tips
you give in your column. It really helped to get
me started.

Jeannie
Latrobe, PA

Dear Jeanie,
Congratulations on your Triple Play discount.
We hope that other new couponers and refunders
will be inspired by your money-saving.

Expiration Dates

Dear Supermarket Shopper:
When you list an expiration date at the end
of your refund listings does this mean the date
when the manufacturer must receive my refund
request letter or is it the date on which I must get
the envelope to the post office?

Roberta S.
Little Rock, AR

Dear Roberta,
Most manufacturers require that your request
for a refund be postmarked no later than the
expiration date. I usually play it safe and mail my
refund request a few days before the offer expires.

15

Trading Refund Forms by Mail

Most experienced refunders trade refund forms by mail. This is one of the secrets of couponing and refunding. A recent survey by the American Coupon Club found that there are more than 50,000 refunders who actively trade forms by mail.

So, don't complain about not being able to find refund forms in the supermarket. Pay close attention to everything in this chapter and you will soon be able to build a collection of many hundreds of refunds forms.

If you send out at least two trades each week, this should provide you with eighty to one hundred new refund forms each month. Trading with refunders in other cities will substantially broaden the variety of refund forms that are available to you.

"Where do I find a trading partner?"

Remember that old neighbor who moved to St. Louis? Why not start with her. Write to her explaining your interest in refunds and offer to trade forms with her. Trading by mail is a great way to renew old acquaintances.

What about your relatives who live in other states? With more people getting "refund fever," it's possible that they are already interested, and will welcome your offer to trade forms.

Here are some of the rules that experienced refunders follow when trading forms by mail:

- Trades are usually made in batches of twenty refund forms. You send out twenty refund forms, your trading pal will send twenty back to you.
- Trades are made on the basis of one-for-one (1-4-1) regardless of value. Since you are trading duplicate forms which have no real value to you, it doesn't matter that you are sending several $1 refund forms and your trading pal may send back a bunch of 50¢ forms.
- The forms you send for trading should be all different. You can expect that your partner will send you all different forms, no duplicates!
- Most important, the forms you send should have at least thirty days before they expire *when they reach your trading partner*. This means that you must put them in the mail at least thirty-five days before they expire. Some traders ask for longer expirations such as forty-five days or even sixty days.
- Refunders don't trade money-plus offers, sweepstakes offers, or cashoff coupons. No matter how good you think the coupon is, don't put it in your trade.
- SASE or EPOP? Many refund form traders ask that you send a self-addressed stamped envelope with your trade. Although this is a common practice, it means that you are paying for postage both ways. A growing number of refunders are following a policy of EPOP, each pays own postage. You send your refund forms to your trading pal, who takes care of mailing the new forms back to you.
- Be sure to put sufficient postage on your envelope. There is nothing as maddening as receiving an envelope full of forms that also has postage due. You can imagine the quality of forms that a postage-due trader gets in return!

An envelope with twenty refund forms and an SASE usually weighs more than one ounce. At current postal rates this requires 28¢ for first-class postage. You can mail up to two ounces third class for 20¢.

• When you receive a trade in the mail, try to respond to it within forty-eight hours. Handling your trades promptly is a courtesy that all refunders appreciate.

A.C.C. Classified Ads

The American Coupon Club's monthly magazine, *The National Supermarket Shopper*, features a large classified ad section for refunders who are interested in exchanging refunds forms by mail. The following is an example of a typical ad:

> TRADE FORMS, 1-4-1, 30 day expiration.
> No cigarettes, money-plus or sweepstakes.
> SASE. Jackie Smith, Smithtown, AR 00000

This advertiser is interested in trading refund forms on a one-for-one basis. All forms sent to the advertiser must have at least thirty days left before they expire. The advertiser is not interested in refunds forms for cigarettes, in forms that offer merchandise for money-plus proofs of purchases, or sweepstakes entry forms. This advertiser wants you to send along a self-addressed stamped envelope with your forms (SASE).

You will also find language in classified ads that may not be familiar to you. Here are some common examples:

Quality for quality

—The advertiser who uses these words is indicating concern with the quality of the forms that you send, and is warning you that you will receive forms that are roughly equivalent in quality to the ones you send out. If you send good quality forms for food, that is what you will get in return. If you send a lot of commonly circulated forms for paper towels and cleaning products, you can expect to get back forms of that type.

No Junk!

—Many novice refunders who don't have good duplicates to trade may resort to "junk" in order to fill their envelopes. What is junk? It's really hard to say. One refunder's idea of junk may be just what another refunder needs. I always considered forms for chewing tobacco junk, but I recently found someone who uses it.

It is a good idea to take a look at the refund forms you are about to send off for a trade and see whether you have more than one cat food form, or cigarette form, or forms for mouthwash or vitamins. If you do, your trading partner may get the feeling that you are sending junk, and certainly this impression should be avoided.

Good anytime—

The advertiser is indicating that the ad will be good for many months.

Limit 15

This is the limit on the number of refund forms that the advertiser will accept for trading.

Cash Forms Only—

This limits the trade to forms that offer cash refunds.

Request Lists Welcome—

Most advertisers will try to fill your requests for specific refund forms. They may in turn send you a request list of their own.

Request Lists

Experienced refunders trade forms by choice and not by chance. They accomplish this by including a request list with every trade they send out.

By trading regularly and using a request list, you

too can obtain almost any form you're looking for within a relatively short time.

It is easy to make a request list of ten to twenty refund forms. You can do it with the help of the refund offers listed in this book. Just go through the listings and check off those that are most appealing to you. They will probably be for products you already use, or could use if you had the incentive of a money-saving refund.

---

refund form trading letter

FROM: _____
_____
_____

TO: _____
_____ DATE: _____
_____ ZIP: _____

I saw your ad offering to trade refund forms. Enclosed are _____ good refund forms with at least 30 days to expiration. Please send me _____ good forms in return. No sweepstakes, or money plus offers.

Sincerely yours.

_____

P.S.
Please include the following forms if you have them:

_____ _____
_____ _____
_____ _____
_____ _____
_____ _____
_____ _____

Be sure to send along a self-addressed, stamped envelope (SASE).
Copyright 1979 American Coupon Club, Inc.
P.O. Box 1149 Great Neck, New York 11023

A Refund Form Trading Letter makes it easy to trade refund forms by mail. Just fill in the blank spaces and send it with your refund forms. Note the section on the bottom for requests.

Refund Robins

One of the best ways to trade refund forms by mail is with a refund robin. A robin is economical because you only pay postage one way, and it can bring you a wide variety of forms from different areas of the country. Most robins require little effort once they get started, and they are a dependable source of forms; every two weeks or so, like clockwork, your robin envelope appears in the mail.

Here is how a refund robin works: It is usually organized by one refunder who asks four other refunders to participate. The organizer of the robin makes a list of the participants, putting her name at the top as number one, and numbering the others #2–#5 in descending order. The organizer, #1, puts the list of participants and five refund forms (with her number on each) in the robin envelope and sends it to participant #2.

On the first time around, participants put into the robin envelope five forms (with their number on each), but they can also take out any forms they find interesting. When a participant takes out a form, it must be replaced with a new form of equal quality, and marked with the same participant number as the one taken out. Participant #2 sends the robin envelope to #3, and #3 to #4 and #4 to #5. At the end of the first round, there should be twenty-five forms in the robin envelope and this should continue as long as there are five participants in the robin.

When the robin envelope returns to #1 after the first round, #1 first takes out the five forms with her number on them, and puts in five new forms, again placing her #1 on each of them. Next, she looks through the twenty other forms, taking those she needs and replacing them with others. Then #1 sends the envelope to #2 and the robin continues in this way

If you want to drop out of a robin, take the five forms with your numbers on them, cross your name off the list, and then send the robin envelope to the next participant on the list. When the envelope returns to the organizer, #1, it is usually up to her to invite another refunder into the robin.

A refund robin is only as good as the refunders who are in it, and their willingness to contribute good quality refund forms. Participants should make a special effort to put into the robin envelope the kind of refund forms they would like to receive. The same trading by mail rules apply: no money-plus, no sweepstakes, and no junk. The robin organizer can also set reasonable rules concerning the types of forms that can be put into the robin. The rules of the robin should be clearly written on the same sheet with the names and addresses of the participants.

You can start a robin with friends in other cities, or suggest a robin to refunders who advertise in the A.C.C. club magazine. Occasionally you will find classified ads from those wishing to start a refund robin.

Here are the usual instructions that are included with the list of robin participants:

First round

1. Put into the robin five good refund forms with your number written on the lower right hand corner of each form.
2. Take out any form you need and replace it with one of equal quality—be sure to write the

participant's number on the form you took out on the form you put back in.
3. Send the contents of the envelope to the next participant.

Second and subsequent rounds:

1. Take out the five forms with your number on them and replace them with five new forms.
2. Take out any other forms you need and replace them with forms of equal quality—again, be sure to put the same number on the forms you put in as the number on the forms you took out.
3. Send the contents of the envelope to the next participant.

If you want to drop out of the robin:

1. Take out the five forms with your number.
2. Cross out your name on the list of participants.
3. Send the contents of the envelope to the next participant.

General robin rules:

1. Do not put into the robin duplicates of any form already in the envelope.
2. Forms must have at least thirty days before expiration when you put them into the robin.
3. Send the contents of the envelope by first class mail to the next participant within two days after you receive it.

Refund Form Chain Letters

Chain letters are illegal even if they require refund forms rather than money. A refund form chain letter usually asks you to send refund forms to the name at the top of a list and then send out similar letters adding your name to the bottom. If you receive this kind of letter throw it out. It is definitely a waste of time and refund forms.

The only chain letter that I have seen that was worth reading is this one:

Dear Friend:

This chain letter was started by a woman like yourself in hopes of bringing relief to tired, discontented women. Unlike most chain letters, this does not cost anything. Send a copy of this letter to 5 friends who are equally tired, disgusted and distraught. Then bundle up your husband and send him to the woman who is at the top of the list, and add your name to the bottom of the list. When your name comes to the top of the list, you will receive 16,475 men and some of them are real dandies. Have faith and don't break the chain. One woman did and she got her own son-of-a-gun back!

> *Sincerely,*
> *A Misunderstood and*
> *Discontented Wife*

P.S. At the time of this writing, a friend of mine had received 165 men. They buried her yesterday, but it took 3 undertakers 36 hours to take the grin off her face.

"How can I trade if I can't find any refund forms?"

You do have a problem in trading forms by mail if you can't find any forms to start with. But the A.C.C. can help new traders. *The National Supermarket Shopper* has a special classified ad section for beginners. In it you will find refunders who will get you started with a supply of refund forms for a small handling charge, never more than $1. Investing a few dollars in refund forms is a quick and relatively inexpensive way to get started.

The "Avid" Form Trader

Once you get started trading by mail, you may find it so interesting and rewarding that you will send out many more trades than the two a week recommended by the A.C.C.

The avid form trader sends out as many as a dozen

trades each week—every one with a request list. Many hours are spent sorting refund forms and fulfilling the requests of other refunders. The result is a collection of several hundred refund forms. This is the kind of collection that allows the refunder to take advantage of a maximum number of refund offers. In return, the refunder receives as much as $100 a month in refund checks and free products.

Is it worth the effort? You bet it is!

The Form Traders Golden Rule

Here is a trading rule well worth following: *"Do unto other form traders as you would have them do unto you."*

REFUNDER'S TRADING RECORD

Trade Sent to	Forms Sent	Date Sent	Date Rec'd	Comments/Notes

REFUNDER'S TRADING RECORD

Trade Sent to	Forms Sent	Date Sent	Date Rec'd	Comments/Notes

16

Coupon Clubs

What do you do with cigarette coupons if you don't smoke, or dog food coupons if you have a cat?

What do you do with Maxwell House refund forms if you drink Sanka, or a Bran Chex form if your kids prefer Wheaties?

You trade them, of course! And the easiest place to trade your unwanted coupons and refund forms is at a coupon club meeting or a swap session.

A swap session is an informal get together where a few friends and neighbors can do some trading. It is easy to start a swap session. All you have to do is pick up the phone and invite a few people over for a cup of coffee. Don't forget to ask them to bring along some coupons and refund forms to swap.

Coupon clubs have regularly scheduled meetings. Most clubs meet once a month, in the evening, at the home of one of the members.

Coupon clubs usually have several dozen members and fifteen to twenty-five generally show up for a meeting. The larger clubs offer a greater selection of coupons and forms and more trading opportunities.

Club meetings usually follow a program that gives each member important couponing and refunding information, an opportunity to trade effectively, and a chance to socialize. Some clubs have other interesting activities and get involved in worthwhile projects.

"How can I find a coupon club near me?"

The American Coupon Club is chartering local coupon clubs in all parts of the country. These clubs are called "A.C.C. Shoppers' Circles." Each month the Club's magazine publishes a list of Shoppers' Circles and the name, address, and phone contact for each club. Readers of this guide who are interested in finding out if there is a Shoppers' Circle near them can inquire by sending a large, stamped, self-addressed envelope to: A.C.C. Shoppers' Circle, Dept. BG-1, P.O. Box 1149, Great Neck, N.Y. 11023.

There are approximately 1,000 local coupon clubs that have no national affiliation. The best way to find one of these clubs is to ask around. Other refunders in your area may know of a club. The food or woman's page editor of your local newspaper may have heard of one. The supermarket managers may be able to put you in contact with a club. You may want to try putting up a note on the supermarket bulletin board, "Looking for a Coupon Club or Swap Session."

Start Your Own Coupon Club!

If there is no coupon club in your area, then you should consider starting one yourself. A good coupon club can multiply your supermarket savings. You can arrive at a meeting with $25 worth of useless coupons and refund forms and after a few fun-filled hours go home with $25 worth of new ones that you can start turning into cash the very next morning.

It is easy to start a club and have successful meetings if you follow the recommendations of the American Coupon Club. The following is a summary of the advice it gives to those couponers and refunders who are interested in starting an A.C.C. Shoppers' Circle.

Planning Your First Meeting

Pick a date for your first meeting. Select one that

is three or four weeks ahead so that you will have plenty of time to spread the word and get organized. A weeknight is usually best and 8 o'clock is an hour that is good for most people.

How do you let people know about your first club meeting? Here are a few ways:

• Spread the message by word of mouth. Tell your friends and ask them to tell others.

• Put up a few bulletin board signs in the supermarkets near you. All the sign needs to say is "NEW COUPON CLUB BEING FORMED. Call (*your first name*) for information," then list your phone number. If there is no bulletin board, ask the manager if you can put the sign in one of his windows. You may also want to post these signs at the public library and other public places where it will be noticed.

• Speak to the food page or woman's page editor of your local newspaper or whomever is in charge of community announcements. They may be interested in publishing the notice of your meeting and it won't cost you a thing. If they can't do it, consider taking a small classified ad. You can use the same brief language as your bulletin board sign.

Have paper and pencil ready so that you can make a list of names and phone numbers when people begin calling for information. Don't try to tell them too much about the meeting, only that the purpose is to trade cashoff coupons and refund forms, and that they will have a good time. Be sure to give accurate and easy-to-follow directions. If they have no experience, assure them that there will be a special class for new couponers and refunders. Remind them to bring unwanted cashoffs and duplicate refund forms and also a large white envelope.

How many people should you have at your first meeting? The American Coupon Club recommends that you have between fifteen and twenty. A group this size is small enough to control comfortably and large enough to do some very worthwhile trading. So, when people start calling, give out the meeting information to the first twenty-five or thirty who say that they will attend (some won't show up), and politely tell the rest that you are putting their names on a special list and you will call them if others inform you that they can't attend.

There are a few things that you will need at the meeting that you should plan for in advance. Purchase or make up some name tags. They make it a lot easier to socialize and learn everyone's name. Plan to serve coffee. You may also want to offer cookies or cake. Be sure you have enough chairs.

Making Your First Meeting a Successful One

Here are the basic parts of a Shoppers' Circle meeting and the order in which they usually occur:

1. Members arrive and sign in. Meeting dues are collected after the first meeting.
2. The meeting begins with a short introduction and special news and announcements from the club sponsor or officer.
3. Next come introductions and show'n'tell from everyone around the circle.
4. Club business is discussed; everyone participates in offering shopping news and couponing and refunding information.
5. Beginners go off to their instruction class.
6. Refund form trading begins, using the Shoppers' Circle method.
7. Members tell which special forms and proofs they are looking for and individual trading begins.
8. Refreshments are served and the meeting is concluded.

Here is the information you need to handle effectively the various parts of the basic Shoppers' Circle meeting:

Starting the Meeting

As members and guests arrive, ask them to sign

in. A piece of lined paper will do. Ask them to clearly print their names, addresses and phone numbers. It is important for you to have this record of who attended your meetings.

At this first meeting you won't be asking for club dues, but members will pay dues at future meetings. Meeting dues are usually $1 or $2 and are paid in cash or complete deals (refund form and required proofs of purchase). Meeting dues are never paid by first-time guests who have not previously attended a Shoppers' Circle meeting.

When members and guests arrive, ask them to sit down and look through their coupons and forms and discard those that have expired. This and a little socializing will keep everyone busy until the meeting actually starts. If your first meeting is like most others, people will begin to arrive a few minutes before the appointed time and then continue to straggle in for the next twenty to thirty minutes. Don't let this bother you. Begin the meeting as promptly as possible.

Start the meeting with a few brief introductory remarks. Thank the members and guests for coming. Tell them that the purpose of the meeting is to help everyone save supermarket dollars through couponing and refunding and that most of the meeting will be devoted to trading coupons and refund forms. Mention that a special class will be given for beginners.

"Show'n'Tell."

This is the inspirational part of the meeting where members show and tell guests and new members how they saved money with their couponing and refunding. For this first meeting you should try to have at least a few experienced refunders tell about some of their best savings experiences. You'll be surprised at how much this inspires beginners and gets the meeting off to a good start. Here are a few ways to do it:

• Pass around a refund check. Many beginners have never seen one before. Tell how you got it and how much of a discount it represents.
• Have someone show a coupon good for a free

product. Explain how it was obtained and how it is turned in at the checkout counter.

• It's fun to show everyone a free product or gift that a manufacturer has sent you, such as a tote bag, a beach towel or a recipe book. Explain where you learned of the offer, how you collected the required proofs, and whether or not you used a refund form when you sent for the item.

• Don't forget to tell about the Double Play and Triple Play discounts you have recently made. Explain them carefully since the beginners won't be familiar with them.

This kind of morale boosting is good not only for beginners but for everyone. People will enjoy talking about their successes and the money they are saving. But don't let the talk get out of hand, especially since the beginners will have many questions to ask. This is where a good leader controls the meeting and asks beginners to hold their questions until the special instruction class.

Since guests and new members won't have much to contribute for Show'n'Tell, ask them to introduce themselves and tell what they hope to achieve through couponing and refunding.

With Show'n'Tell over, it's a good time to give away a door prize. It is fun to have a prize drawing and the sponsor or hostess for the evening usually contributes ten refund forms and a few dollars worth of cashoff coupons as the door prize. You can select the winner from a grab bag, if you have put numbers in the bag that correspond to numbers on your sign-in sheet or on the name tags you have given out. Be sure to have the drawing for the door prize at this time rather than at the end of the meeting because it encourages everyone to come on time.

Announcements, Club Business, Shopping News

It is now time to make announcements. Shopper's Circle sponsors and officers receive a Briefing Bulletin containing important and valuable information that should be passed along to members at this time.

Club business comes next. A new club may not have much business to transact, but as you will see further on in this chapter, clubs can become involved in a variety of activities that require discussion among their members. When it is "News Time" members are asked to give any news they may have about where to find new refund forms, which stores are having the best sales, and which ones are offering double coupon savings. This is also the time when any member who has something to sell or give away, tells the other members about it. Don't forget to announce the time and place of the next meeting.

Beginners' Instruction Class

You are now ready to ask the beginners to move to another part of the room, or if possible to another room, for their class in couponing and refunding. Beginners shouldn't be left on their own to learn about couponing and refunding in bits and pieces. It is essential that you or another experienced refunder take them aside and teach them some of the basics. After the class begins, the experienced refunders can start their Shoppers' Circle trading session.

We don't have enough room in this chapter to set forth in detail the essentials that beginners should learn at their first coupon club meeting. But, having read this far, you already know enough about couponing and refunding to explain the basic parts and some of the secrets of success.

First, explain how cashoff coupons are separated into the twelve A.C.C. product groups. Next, tell them about the thousands of refund offers manufacturers make each year. They will ask you why they don't see more of them and you should be able to give them a good answer. You should also be prepared to tell them all the ways that experienced refunders find the forms they need: at club meetings like this one and by trading refund forms by mail. Explain to them why it is important to save every possible proof of purchase —everything! Show them how to use the Clip'n File refund listings to make a request list. Last but not least, tell them about this book which will help to answer most of their questions about couponing and refunding.

You will also help beginners by carefully and patiently answering their many questions. When you have explained the basics and answered questions, the beginners are ready to start a trading circle of their own.

Trading Forms

Trading refund forms can be a disorganized affair which takes some of the fun out of a club meeting. If coupon traders are left to their own devices, some people move around and trade a lot. Others are uncertain of what they are doing; they stay in the background and do little productive trading. But this isn't the way Shoppers' Circle members trade forms.

The Shoppers' Circle way of trading is very simple: The members form a circle and each person puts fifteen or twenty different refund forms in an envelope with their name on the outside. Money-plus and sweepstakes forms should not be used. The trading starts with everyone passing an envelope to the person on the left. Each member now has two minutes to look through the forms in the envelope, take out the ones needed, and replace them with forms of approximately equal quality. When the two minutes are up, whoever is doing the timing (you can use an egg timer) calls out "Pass your forms to the left." The envelopes keep moving around the circle in this way until each member gets back the original envelope with their name on it. With twenty or more people at a meeting, you are sure to find at least twenty worthwhile forms in other members' envelopes and as many as fifteen new ones in your own.

It takes about an hour to go around the circle, but everyone gets an equal chance to trade forms and increase refunding opportunities. And most important, there is no hassle about whether your form is worth as much as my form.

When the beginners are through with their class,

show them the shoppers' circle method of trading, and get them started with their own small trading circle.

Getting the Right Forms, POPs and Cashoff Coupons

It is now time to do some individual trading. Some Shoppers' Circles start this off by letting members tell the group which special forms, proofs of purchase and cashoffs they are looking for. Some members find it helpful to take notes so that they can remember which members are looking for items that they have.

Refund forms are usually traded one-for-one for those of approximately the same value and quality. But exceptions are made for very high value refund forms and those forms that are very difficult to find. In these cases a member with such a form may want several forms in exchange.

There is no general rule for trading proofs of purchase that are needed for current refund offers. Each proof may be worth one refund form or twenty refund forms depending on the value of the offer for which they are needed. Run-of-the-mill proofs from national brand products are usually sold in batches of fifty or one hundred for a penny or two each.

Many couponers are very casual about trading their cashoff coupons. If the cashoffs are for products the couponers don't use, they may invite other members to pick out any that they need, and in turn they are given the opportunity to do the same from the other members' cashoffs. A growing number of couponers are putting their cashoffs in $1 and $2 batches by product group and offering to trade them for like amounts of other product group cashoffs. The rule here is that there should be no duplicates in each batch and that each cashoff must have at least two weeks before it expires.

Socializing

When the members start individual trading, it is time to serve the coffee and cake. As the trading begins to taper off, the socializing will pick up. At some clubs the refreshment costs are part of the meeting dues. At others, different members bring the cake to each meeting and the person at whose home the meeting is held supplies the coffee.

The American Coupon Club recommends that your Shoppers' Circle meeting end by 11 p.m. You will find that there are some members who would gladly stay until midnight if you would let them, but it makes sense to wrap up the meeting before it gets too late. Be sure that those who arrived late sign in so you can contact them about the next meeting.

Making Your Club Meetings More Exciting and Worthwhile

There should be more to a good club meeting than just trading coupons and refund forms. Of course, the trading sessions are the basic reason why you join a coupon club, but there is much more that a good club can do to add interest and excitement to its meetings. Here are a few suggestions for enlivening your coupon club meeting:

Comparison shopping can save every club member supermarket dollars. At each meeting five or six members can report on prices at the supermarkets where they usually shop. They can easily do this if the club prints a one-page form listing a few basic items in each of the important supermarket product categories. At the meeting, one of the members can read off the items on this list, and the other comparison shoppers can make comments when their prices are higher or lower. It is an interesting exercise in smart shopping and members are often surprised by the price differences among stores.

Clubs can make their meetings more fun by running contests and games that test the couponing and refunding skill of their members. A "Contest and Games Committee" can plan a refund-form treasure hunt, or offer a prize for the member who brings in the largest manufacturer's refund check at the next meeting. Prizes can be refund forms from the club collection, or a coupon wallet, or something that the club can purchase with money from its treasury.

Club treasury? Yes, a coupon club should have a

treasury. Members can be asked to contribute as little as 25¢ at each meeting, or even as much as a dollar if the club's plans are ambitious. These monies can be used to provide contest prizes and special refreshments, or to pay for a club outing or a special members' dinner. The many ways that a club treasury can be used are limited only by the imaginations and pocketbooks of its members.

An active coupon club can also increase its members' savings by doing some co-operative buying. A club that arranges to purchase food in case lots can save members as much as 20 percent. Clubs that become known in the community may find it possible to obtain special discounts for their members. For example, a discount may be offered to club members who shop early in the week when the stores most need their business. A "Club Purchasing Committee" should contact store owners and managers to inquire about case-lot discounts and special discounts for members.

Contacts with local supermarkets also helps when club members encounter difficulties such as a store that is consistently out of stock on advertised specials and refuses to give rain checks. If the club has had previous contact with the store management, it may be easier to resolve such problems. A call from a club sponsor or officer may be all that is required to get action. But, when polite measures are met with indifference, club members should consider other steps, such as directing complaints to local and state consumer protection agencies; calling newspaper, radio, and television action lines; and if necessary, parading in front of the store with signs and placards. A good coupon club takes these matters seriously and stands up for the rights of its members.

Many clubs have set up an "Education Committee." One of the functions of this committee is to provide club members as speakers for home economics classes, senior citizens groups, and other organizations interested in learning how to save money with coupons and refunds. This type of service activity helps to establish a club's identity, reputation, and prestige in the community.

The American Coupon Club urges its Shoppers' Circles to aid a worthy cause with their refunds. The contribution by each member of one refund at each meeting from September to December, can provide Christmas baskets for the needy. A club can even adopt an orphan overseas with its contributions. These are just two examples of ways that clubs can make couponing and refunding satisfying as well as money saving.

Once every three or four months, clubs should plan to hold joint meetings with other clubs. These events allow club members to make new friends and broaden their couponing and refunding contacts.

Comparison shopping, contests, club trips and dinners, group purchasing, helping members with shopping problems, and community service are just a few of the many ways that members of a coupon club can make meetings more exciting and worthwhile. These are the kinds of activities that club members eagerly anticipate.

A.C.C. Shoppers' Circles

Participating in an active A.C.C. Shoppers' Circle multiplies your enjoyment of couponing and refunding and is guaranteed to increase your money saving opportunities. The American Coupon Club therefore urges its members to join a Shoppers' Circle or start one of their own.

Strong A.C.C. Support

The American Coupon Club supports its Shoppers' Circles in many ways. First, the A.C.C. provides each club with a charter and bylaws. This assures that each club will conduct its activities in an orderly, ethical, and productive manner. The sponsor or organizing officer of each new club receives a kit that includes supermarket bulletin board signs, local press releases, and reprints from the series of articles "How to Start a Coupon Club." Club leaders periodically receive a Briefing Bulletin, and each club is listed in *The National Supermarket Shopper*.

Club Listings

Each month *The National Supermarket Shopper* publishes a complete listing of all Shoppers' Circle coupon clubs. The listing includes the name and phone number of the person who can be contacted for information. This year many thousands of interested couponers and refunders will look through these listings to find a club near them. Plans are being made for an annual club directory that will be available to the general public.

Briefing Bulletin

The A.C.C. periodically sends sponsors or club officers an *A.C.C. Shoppers' Circle Briefing Bulletin*. This bulletin contains special information that should be passed along to club members. The Briefing Bulletin is a vital link between the A.C.C. national organization and the local clubs. The bulletin will often ask for information from club members concerning their opinions and preferences. When action is needed to protect the rights and interests of supermarket shoppers, the bulletin is the fastest way for the club to communicate with its members. As the number of Shoppers' Circles grows from the hundreds to the thousands, these clubs will have an important impact on both supermarkets and manufacturers.

Club Activities

The A.C.C. provides Shoppers' Circles with advice on activity and program planning: how to run club contests, how to find interesting speakers for meetings, how to plan a city-wide swap session. *The National Supermarket Shopper* reports on the most interesting of these club activities and events.

With Shoppers' Circles being formed all over the United States, planning has already started for state and national coupon and refund conventions and a variety of exciting special events.

Shopper Grievances

Shoppers' Circles are expected to take an active role in helping members who have been treated unfairly by stores, supermarkets, and manufacturers. To assist them, the A.C.C. is publishing its guidelines for local action. In those instances where local clubs do not have the ability to solve these problems, the A.C.C., working on a national level and communicating directly with executives and officers of chains and manufacturers, will do everything possible to redress these grievances.

Sponsored and Hosted Clubs

A.C.C. Shoppers' Circles are organized in one of two ways: the first is a sponsored club, where the organizer or organizers want to retain leadership of the club. There are several reasons why you may want to be a sponsor; one reason is that meeting dues can provide you with an extra source of income. A sponsor usually holds all club meetings at home and leads the activities. It is possible for one person to be the sponsor of several Shoppers' Circles.

Being a sponsor requires that you be a good leader and enjoy working with people. If the organizer of a club does not want to have these responsibilities on a permanent basis, then it might be preferable to set up the club as a hosted club. A hosted club elects officers who assume leadership responsibilities for the club and its activities. Hosted clubs usually meet at the home of a different member each month, and that member receives the meeting dues.

You don't have to decide how you want to organize the club until after you have received your initial Shoppers' Circle package of information. Whichever form you decide on, it's fun to start a Shoppers' Circle and certainly well worth the effort.

Register As a Shopper's Circle

If you would like to organize an A.C.C. Shoppers' Circle, or if you already have a group that would like to become a Shoppers' Circle, the cost for a full year's registration is only $6. You must be a member of the American Coupon Club in order to register a Shoppers' Circle and all new members of the Circle must join the A.C.C.

Your $6 registration fee gives your club its charter and bylaws, your club organizing kit, a monthly listing in *The National Supermarket Shopper,* assistance with problems that affect your members, the Briefing Bulletin and a lot more. It is a great deal of help and support for very little money.

To register your Shoppers' Circle, make out a check for $6 to the American Coupon Club and send it with the application form below to: A.C.C. Shoppers' Circles, P.O. Box 1149, Great Neck, N.Y. 11023. Fill in the location of the club as you would like it listed in *The National Supermarket Shopper,* and the name and phone number of a person who will give information to those who inquire. That's all it takes, so send in your application today.

SHOPPER'S CIRCLE APPLICATION

Please register our group as an A.C.C. Shopper's Circle. Enclosed is our $6 registration fee. Send us our Charter and By-Laws, and information kit on starting a coupon club.

Name of Organizer _____

Address _____

City/State/Zip _____

Telephone Contact _____

Club Location _____

17

Conventions

What is a refunder's convention?

Is it fun? Can you really spend an entire week-end thinking about coupons and refund forms?

The best way to answer these questions is to tell you about the 7th Annual Pennsylvania Refunder's Convention. This convention, one of the biggest and best in the nation, was held at a luxurious mountain resort in Pennsylvania.

More than 275 avid couponers and refunders at-

THIS CARD IS TO CONFIRM YOUR

RESERVATION
FOR THE **VOID**
PA. REFUNDERS' CONVENTION

Friday & Saturday, August 17-18, 1979

AT·SEVEN SPRINGS MOUNTAIN RESORT
CHAMPION, PENNSYLVANIA

(This Card Must Be Presented At Door)

tended the convention. They came from fourteen states and from as far away as Phoenix and Miami. Although the majority of the conventioneers were from Pennsylvania, New York, Ohio and Maryland were also well represented.

Convention activities were scheduled to begin on Friday evening with a 6 p.m. trading session. At 5:30 I joined several dozen fellow coupon clippers waiting for the doors to the convention hall to open. There was an air of suppressed excitement as we waited for the big moment to arrive. I remembered having the same feeling just before I got off the plane in Las Vegas.

At 6 p.m. the doors swung open and we all streamed into the convention hall. Long tables had been arranged in several rows running the length of the hall. Everyone quickly found a spot and started to unload coupons and refund forms. Some couponers had their whole trading collection in a few envelopes or a scrapbook. But many others were busy taking coupons and forms out of large cartons and suitcases.

The hall was soon buzzing with trading activity. Traders moved from chair to chair and from table to table.

"I want this Ziploc form," I heard on one side of me.

"Do you have any Pringles proofs?" someone else asked.

I saw a refund form that I had never seen before. I laid out some of my better forms and a trade was quickly made.

I moved to another table and sat down at an empty chair. Picking up a scrapbook, I started thumbing through its pages. It only takes a minute or two to look through a hundred or more forms. If there is nothing interesting you move on.

I traded with Pat Santillo from Rochester, New York. She told me about her large collection of proofs of purchase. "It's a very poor parking lot that doesn't give you something," she said.

Time passed quickly and the trading session was still going strong when I broke away and headed for a party given by the convention organizers Mary Trimbath and Rosemary Mehall. It turned out to be a warm and friendly get-together where it was easy to strike up a conversation and make friends. We heard many stories, like the one from Sandy Wojcik from Cairnbrook, Pennsylvania: She and her family were on a camping trip when she spotted a Nestlé wrapper floating downstream. She thought she needed it for a refund and sent her husband into neck-deep water to retrieve it!

I also heard about another poor fellow who opened the door to the family linen closet and was completely buried under an avalanche of Kleenex boxes. Luckily for him, the UPC codes had been cut from the boxes and there was a little room for him to breathe!

At midnight the traders in the convention hall were reluctantly packing up their refund forms. But they quickly rushed back to their rooms to resume trading. The doors to the rooms were opened, and anyone was welcome to walk in and join the fun.

Can you picture coupon clippers toting suitcases full of coupons and forms through hotel hallways at 3 a.m. in the morning? At 4 a.m. I finally called it quits.

At 8:30 the next morning I was on line filling my plate at the breakfast buffet. I sat down and had breakfast with some refunders from the Pittsburgh area. They told me about the "Rich lady" from Westmont who once a week puts on rubber gloves and hip boots and wades into the town garbage dump looking for labels and other proofs of purchase.

Convention activities resumed at 9 a.m. with a refunding seminar. I joined several other speakers in making a presentation of the latest refunding information. Joe Neuberger described his interesting tour of the refund clearing house in Maple Plain, Minnesota.

After the presentations, there were lots of questions from the large audience:

"Why was the Underwood 6/30/80 offer being returned 'box closed'?" It was a mistake and you can send your proofs in again.

"I have a refund form for Chef's Surprise. Is it still being made?" No, and there are other forms floating around for products that are no longer being made, such as Green Earth, Recipe Dry Dog Food, and Kraft Pizza Mix.

There were questions about duplicate refund requests, about the length of time it takes to receive refunds, and about rejection letters.

Soon it was lunchtime and we sat down with Mary Trimbath and Rosemary Mehall to find out what it was like to put on such a well-organized convention. They recounted their labors.

"More than a year's planning."

"Attention to hundreds of details."

"A lot of hard work."

They smiled as they recounted their labors. Obviously it was well worth the effort.

The afternoon seminar featured a Philadelphia lawyer who is, himself, a refunder. He is very aggressive about his refunding and the way in which he shops. Everyone enjoyed his presentation. He then answered questions: "Are refunds taxable?" Not if you receive less than you paid for the product. "Are you allowed to trade or sell cashoff coupons?" Yes! You purchased the newspaper that carried them and they are yours to do with as you please.

At 3 p.m. the seminar was over.

Did we all head for the swimming pool or the tennis courts?

NO! Out came the scrapbooks, boxes, and suitcases. It was trading time again!

During the afternoon I asked many of my trading partners how long they had been refunding and how much they were saving. Emma Daniels of Mt. Pleasant, Pennsylvania, said that she has been refunding since 1972. Her best year brought her more than $1,000 in refunds and $600 in free products.

Iris Pearce of Philipsburg, Pennsylvania, said that she is saving more than $100 a month. Gloria Colon, an A.C.C. member from Bethlehem, Pennsylvania, told us that she saves $80 a month, and she works full time! Maggie Hanerfeld from Potomac, Maryland, said that her cashoffs and refunds save her more than $100 a month. We heard similar reports from many others.

The convention banquet on Saturday evening featured a double buffet that stretched for more than sixty feet. There were over a hundred mouth-watering dishes, and at the end of the buffet stood a chef in a high white hat, carving from a huge roast beef. As the dinner came to an end, Mary Trimbath and Rosemary Mehall received a standing ovation and they certainly deserved it.

Was the convention over? Would I fulfill my promise to get a good night's sleep? No luck! Back on the ninth and tenth floors, doors were thrown open and we started trading again. Many of my fellow traders were adding up their new coupons and refund forms. For some of the big traders, this would be a free weekend!

On Sunday morning I packed my bags and got ready to leave for home. As I walked down the hallway with my luggage, I heard peals of laughter coming from the maids' supply room. There, standing inside the supply room, were three refunders from Ohio who had made friends with the hotel maids. They were happily stripping the White Cloud wrappers off a whole room full of toilet tissue!

What do you do at a refunder's convention? You have a ball!

For many of the refunders who came to the Pennsylvania convention, this was their third or fourth trip back, and they look forward to coming again next year.

I do too!

Here are answers to the most frequently asked questions about coupon and refund conventions:

"Do conventions usually last for a full weekend?"

No, many conventions are one-day affairs: A couponing and refunding seminar in the morning and a trading session in the afternoon. As convention organizers become more experienced, they tend to make their conventions longer and more elaborate.

"Who can attend a convention?"

Most conventions are open to all couponers and

refunders. Some require advance registration, others allow you to register at the door.

"Is there a charge to attend?"

There is usually a registration fee. The amount of the fee depends on the length of the convention, the place where it is held, and the refreshments and meals that may be included. The registration fee for the Pennsylvania Refunders Convention was about $20; this included all the weekend activities, the party, and the banquet dinner. All things considered, it was a real bargain. The hotel accommodations were of course additional.

"How can I find out when and where future conventions will be held?"

The National Supermarket Shopper publishes announcements of coupon and refund conventions. The conventions are usually held in the Spring and Fall.

"Does anyone provide information on how to put on a convention?"

The American Coupon Club has a new booklet "How to Hold a Couponers and Refunders Convention." It is available to any member of an A.C.C. Shoppers' Circle coupon club.

18

The American Coupon Club

The primary objective of the American Coupon Club is to help supermarket shoppers save money. The Club accomplishes this by providing its members with special information and services. The A.C.C. also provides guidance and support to local Shoppers' Circle coupon clubs. In addition, the A.C.C. is working for the enactment of protective consumer legislation that has a direct impact on supermarket shoppers all across the nation.

The A.C.C. Provides Information and Services to Its Members

The very best source for learning of the thousands of refund offers that manufacturers make each year is *The National Supermarket Shopper,* the monthly magazine sent to all A.C.C. members. Each month, members receive money-saving information on more than 200 new refund offers—more than 2400 new offers each year! These refund offers are arranged according to the A.C.C.'s twelve product groups and printed in Clip'n File lists that are used with cashoff coupons to spot Double Play discounts.

Each issue of *The Shopper* contains a long list of Refund Forms To Write For; a list of SMPs, the specially marked packages that contain coupons and refund forms; a survey of cashoff coupons and the discounts they provide; a national survey of sale-priced supermarket specials showing the tremendous savings that can be obtained by shopping for these specials; a long list of current Double Play discounts, the kind that saves you 40 to 65 percent; and a special reference section that provides the beginner with basic couponing and refunding information. You will also find a fully illustrated Triple Play discount to show you that it isn't hard to find these big discount opportunities. Free Offers, Dollar Stretcher tips, you will find them all in *The Shopper*.

The A.C.C. receives hundreds of letters each week from members who have questions or want help with their problems. The most interesting of these letters are published in Letters to Ruth Brooks, one of the most popular features of *The Supermarket Shopper*. Each month you will also find stories and articles of special interest to couponers, refunders, and super-smart shoppers. The first articles on how to start a coupon club and how to form a refund robin, were published in *The Shopper*. Supermarket Roundup gives you a look at the interesting and special things that are happening at supermarkets in various parts of the country. Planning Menus With Coupons and Refunds shows you how experienced refunders feed their families better for a lot less money.

The Shopper also provides very special entertainment for coupon clippers. First, there's a Shopper's Crossword Puzzle, the only one of its kind to include words like Green Giant and Sara Lee! Super Sally is the madcap shopper who will fill your eyes with tears of laughter as she recounts her supermarket adventures. There are supermarket poets, and you will find their favorite works in the Poet's Corner. *The Shopper* also challenges your couponing and refunding skill with a new and exciting contest each month.

The Trading Post is the magazine's classified ad section. In it you will find other refunders who are anxious to trade their refund forms with you, or have you participate in their refund round robins. There are also ads for beginners that offer an initial supply of refund forms.

The National Supermarket Shopper has become an indispensable part of couponing and refunding for all A.C.C. members. Here is what they have to say:

> *I just returned from the grocery store and thanks to the A.C.C. I doubled my savings. Last Friday I was ready to give up. Then I received the* Supermarket Shopper *and Bingo! That very day*

I sat down and read the whole thing—cover to cover. I learned so many things I was overlooking, words can't explain how happy I am tonight.

> Karen Reeds,
> Belvidere, IL

I have used cents-off coupons for years, but never realized all the dollars our garbage can has devoured in the form of labels and boxtops, until I read the A.C.C.'s Supermarket Shopper.

> Jessie Haenisch,
> Arkport, NY

It's all your fault! I quit refunding eight years ago and then I started receiving the A.C.C.'s Supermarket Shopper. *I'm now trading with six people from the classified ads, and the mailman is looking very suspicious at all this new incoming and outgoing mail. Thank you for giving me back a hobby I missed, only now with three children it's more than a hobby. It's nice to come home from shopping and tell my husband how much I have saved instead of how much I spent.*

> Gail Weir,
> Hornell, NY

I've just been couponing and refunding for a few months, but my savings have been as much as $20 a week during that time. I am very excited about the prospects of saving even more.

> Donna Haney,
> Parma, OH

The A.C.C. Provides Guidance and Support to Local Coupon Clubs

A.C.C. Shoppers' Circles bring couponers and re-funders together for both pleasure and profit. Coupon clippers who don't belong to a local coupon club, miss out on all the fun and most of the money-saving opportunities that club meetings offer.

The number of A.C.C. Shoppers' Circles is growing rapidly. Plans are being made for state and national conventions and special events.

You must be a member of the American Coupon Club in order to join a Shoppers' Circle.

The A.C.C. Represents All Supermarket Shoppers

There are many consumer advocates, but the American Coupon Club is the only national organization that exclusively represents the interests of supermarket shoppers.

Here are just a few of the important supermarket issues that the A.C.C. is working on:

• Product labeling: The A.C.C. believes that supermarket shoppers should be able to look at a food package and see the date on which the box, can, or bottle was packaged. Shoppers have a right to know that the food they purchase is freshly packaged.

• Uniform legislation relating to advertised products: If a product is advertised, a shopper should be able to purchase that product at the advertised price, and should have a right to a rain check if it is not available.

• Individual item price markings: The introduction of computerized cash registers gives supermarkets the ability to discontinue putting price markings on each individual item. At present, several states protect shoppers by requiring food stores to put price markings on most of their items. The A.C.C. is working with consumer groups for the enactment of similar legislation in every state.

In the pages of *The National Supermarket Shopper* you will find important articles that reflect a vital concern with the rights and special needs of supermarket shoppers:

• The A.C.C. reported on the good and bad features of the generic no frills products, and told its members why the supermarkets want to get rid of them.

• The A.C.C. uncovered the "Soy-Beef" rip-off and gave members the information they needed to decide whether this product would actually save them money.

In 1980 The American Coupon Club will play a greater role in advocating the rights of supermarket shoppers and in fostering legislation to protect their interests.

A Club In Which Everyone Can Participate

The American Coupon Club depends on its members to provide the vital information necessary for successful couponing and refunding. Each month, members from around the country send the A.C.C. thousands of refund forms. Several hundred of these provide the information used to prepare the Clip'n File refund listings.

Members also send in rejection letters, information on Box Closed offers, and the refund pad cardboards that provide information on where to write for refund forms.

In return for this information, the Club sends its members A.C.C. Gift Point Checks which can be redeemed for any of the hundreds of gifts shown in the A.C.C. Members' Gift Book.

Members also send in letters to Ruth Brooks, articles on couponing, refunding and super-smart shopping, and information on local club activities. When they are published, the A.C.C. awards these members with Gift Point Checks. A.C.C. members also receive 500 gift points for each new member that they introduce to the Club.

Information and services for its members—
Guidance and support to local coupon clubs—
Representing the rights and interests of all supermarket shoppers—

This is what the A.C.C. is all about.

A no risk application for A.C.C. membership is provided for your convenience. The sooner you join, the sooner you will receive the money in the bank benefits of A.C.C. membership.

YOU'RE INVITED TO JOIN
THE AMERICAN COUPON CLUB

---------------◆Application Form◆-----------------

YES! I want to join the Money-Savers.

Please enroll me as a member of
THE AMERICAN COUPON CLUB

Enclosed is $15 dues for a full year membership. I am to receive as my new-member bonus the free classified ads and refund form trading letters. During the year I will enjoy all the benefits of membership and receive 12 issues of **The National Supermarket Shopper** magazine. You will also send me the A.C.C. Member's Gift Catalog so I can earn gifts for sending in new refund forms, stories for the **Shopper** and for introducing new members to the American Coupon Club. I understand that this is a No-Risk offer with a prompt money-back guarantee.

Name _____

Address _____

City _____ State _____ Zip _____

_____

Enclose Payment To:
   American Coupon Club
   Dept. BB-1, Box 1149
   Great Neck, N.Y. 11023
(Please allow approximately 6 weeks to process your membership. $12 of your dues is attributed to receiving the club magazine for a full year.)

No Risk Money Back Guarantee:
If not satisfied, return the first issue of the
Shopper for a prompt and full refund.

19

It's Illegal!

It is unfortunate, but there are some people who aren't satisfied with honest savings or honest earnings. These are the coupon cheats and coupon crooks who misredeem cashoff coupons. What they are doing is illegal and is costing honest shoppers money. Honest shoppers must fight back against this type of criminal activity, or it may grow and endanger our honest savings.

Coupon Fraud

Each year manufacturers lose millions of dollars because of the fraudulent misredemption of cashoff coupons.

The most common type of coupon fraud occurs when a store owner redeems cashoff coupons that haven't been used by shoppers to purchase products.

These coupon crooks conspire to obtain bushel baskets of coupons by any means available. Some have hired school children to operate paper cutters that cut the coupons out of whole piles of newspapers. They then send these coupons to the manufacturer, just as if they had been used by shoppers to purchase the manufacturer's products.

This type of misredemption is a fraud against the manufacturer, and is a criminal offense punishable by fines and imprisonment.

In years past, many store owners felt that no one paid much attention to this kind of petty crime. But this has radically changed. Law enforcement officials throughout the country are now moving aggressively to prosecute these coupon crooks. Their efforts to obtain evidence against them has been aided by the U.S. Postal Service and the manufacturers themselves.

The Breen Story, The Detergent That Never Was

Coupons are usually sent by store owners through the mail to the manufacturers to be redeemed. Because of this, the U.S. Postal Service and its team of crack investigators have taken an active role in hunting down coupon crooks. One of their best known operations involved "Breen," a detergent that never existed.

The idea of using cashoff coupons for a product that didn't exist was conceived by the postal authorities in conjunction with New York City law enforcement officials, and enlisted the cooperation of Blair Marketing, a major distributor of newspaper inserts containing cashoff coupons.

Through the Blair Company's newspaper inserts, several million Breen coupons were distributed over the course of one weekend in three New York area newspapers. Then the postal inspectors and law enforcement authorities sat back and waited.

The Breen coupon instructed grocers who had supposedly given shoppers a 25¢ discount for buying a box of Breen, to send the coupon to Breen at: CFCP Redemption Center, P.O. Box 996, Clinton, Iowa. What these grocers didn't know was that CFCP stood for *Coupon Fraud Control Program,* and that the post office box had actually been rented by the postal inspectors!

The 25¢-off coupon for "New Breen" was printed with the headline that it was "The Detergent That Washes away Dirt and Grime," and it actually helped to wash up into view some of the worst coupon crooks in the New York area. Within a week after they were distributed, the coupons started pouring into the postal inspector's box. Within a few months more than 70,000 Breen coupons had been received for redemption. Most had been sent in by grocers and supermarkets in New Jersey, New York City, and Long Island.

Undercover Work and Then the Raids

Then began an intense surveillance of the stores that had turned in the Breen coupons. Undercover agents were used, many of whom took jobs as supermarket clerks and cashiers so that they would be in a position to see how the stores handled their coupons.

One female Postal Service undercover agent was hired as a clerk by a supermarket chain, and was immediately put to work cutting coupons out of newspapers.

Raids followed the undercover work. Police searching an illegal coupon "clip-house" found more than a million cashoff coupons that had been mass-cut on machines. They were neatly stacked by product in more than 1,400 piles. These coupons, if they had been redeemed, would have cost the manufacturers more than $250,000.

Another raid at the Long Island headquarters of a ten store chain netted the law officers nineteen cartons of coupons as well as forty-seven bundles of uncut newspapers.

Indictments and Arrests

Indictments and arrests quickly followed. Twenty-six Brooklyn merchants were indicted on charges ranging from petty theft to grand larceny. Other indictments followed, including the arrest of many of those who had supplied these coupon crooks with their coupons.

> ## 26 Are Charged In Coupon Fraud
>
> Twenty-six Brooklyn merchants who allegedly defrauded four major coupon-redemption centers of more than $122,000 in one year have been indicted, District Attorney Eugene Gold of Brooklyn announced.
>
> According to the indictment, single proprietors submitted coupons under several fictitious store names, real stores submitted coupons for products never sold and coupon operators provided masses of coupons for a store for a 50 percent kickback.
>
> The District Attorney received evidence of the fraudulent practices by inventing a fake product called "Breen" and by placing coupons for it in newspaper advertisements. Seventy thousand coupons were submitted for redemption by 427 Brooklyn retailers.

To Catch a Crook

Manufacturers are helping to uncover coupon crooks through a variety of means: They are checking their sales records to spot stores that are redeeming more coupons than the goods they purchased. New computers are keeping track of the stores that redeem cashoff coupons; when the computer spots unusual activity, such as a small store turning in a large number of coupons, it alerts the manufacturer. Manufacturers and their agents are also taking more stringent precautions to check the identity of those redeeming cashoff coupons.

These new efforts have proven their effectiveness. As a result, more than one hundred criminal investigations are now under way concerning coupon fraud.

A Warning To Shoppers

Shoppers who sell or otherwise provide cashoff coupons to store owners for the purpose of misredemption, are themselves guilty of a fraudulent act. They are accomplices to the fraud upon the manufacturers, and can be prosecuted along with the store owners. There is an effort now to make examples of such shoppers.

Some coupon crooks try to enlist religious and other groups to clip coupons with an offer to pay them a cent or two for each coupon. One such religious organization in the Los Angeles area, after collecting almost a million coupons, was publicly embarrassed when the crooks they were clipping for were arrested. In the end they received nothing for their efforts.

So take warning: If you or your group are asked by someone to provide them with coupons, beware! Avoid any relationship that could provide cashoff coupons for misredemption.

20

Refund Listings

We want you to start refunding today. The sooner you start refunding, the sooner you will be able to see the savings mount up and refund checks roll in.

To get you off to a good start we have included in this section more than $200 worth of current refund offers. We know that many of the refund offers will be for products you may not be using, but we hope that you will find dozens of refunds that will be of use to you and which will pay you back many times the cost of this book.

There are several ways that you can put these listings to work for you right now:

• Take a red pen and check off all the refunds for products you presently use. If they don't require a refund form, you may already have the required proofs of purchase and you can send for the refund immediately—but please read the last part of this chapter which tells you about sending for your refunds.

• Since the manufacturer is going to pay you back a

part of the purchase price, you might as well be flexible in your choice of products. So, mark off the refunds for products that you could use if you switched brands or wanted to try something new.

● Use the refund listings in this section to make up a refund form request list. Use carbon paper to make several copies. You will be listing most of the offers that you have previously checked off. These lists will be used when you start trading refund forms through the mail.

● Look at these refund listings when you make up your next shopping list. You should start favoring the products that will soon fill your mailbox with refund cash and free products.

How to Read the Refund Listings

It is easy to read the refund listings found in this section because the information you need is always shown in the same order. By the time you have read the first ten refund offers you should have no problem understanding the listings.

—JONE'S APPLE CAKE $1.00 REFUND OFFER, P.O. Box 213, El Paso, TX 79977 ($1) Send 2 POP seals from any variety of Jone's Apple Cakes. (Refund Form Required) 9/30/81

At the upper left is a space you can use to place a check mark when you have obtained the refund form, or to show that you are interested in that offer.

Next comes the name of the refund offer shown in capital letters. This name is also the first line of the address to which you send your refund request. Following the name of the offer you will find the second and third lines of the address.

Occasionally the name of the offer doesn't include the name of the product or the manufacturer. In this case one of the two will be shown in parentheses before the name of the refund offer:

—(JONE'S) APPLE CAKE $1.00 REFUND
OFFER.

Immediately after the name and address of the offer, the listing shows the refund, product, or discount coupon you will receive from the manufacturer. The item you will receive is always shown in parentheses. Here are some common examples of what you will find within the parentheses:

($1) ....This indicates that you will receive a $1 refund. The refund will usually be in the form of a check made out to your name.

(50¢ Cpn.) ....You will receive a fifty cent cashoff store coupon which is usually good on your next purchase of the same product as the proof of purchase required by the offer.

(5/20¢ Cpns.) ....You will receive five 20¢ cashoff coupons, usually for the same product for which you sent proofs of purchase.

(PP of Lettuce
up to 75¢) ....This means that you will receive a store coupon good for up to 75¢ on your next lettuce purchase. If the required proof of purchase is a register receipt on which you have circled the price of the lettuce, then the refund will be a check for the amount circled with a 75¢ limit.

(Package of Rice) ....This tells you that you will receive a coupon that you can redeem at the supermarket for a free package of that manufacturer's product. In this case it is rice.

(50¢–$2.50) ....In this case the refund offer can save you as much as $2.50 or as little as 50¢ depending on the

proofs of purchase you decide
to send in to the manufacturer.

(Free Designer
Tote Bag) ....You will be sent this gift as indicated. In many cases it is sent
directly from the manufacturer
of the gift.

The next part of the refund listing shows you the
required proof or proofs of purchase. This part begins
with the word "Send . . ." Our example asked for two
POP seals from any variety of Jone's Apple Cakes.
This tells you to look at the Jone's Apple Cake boxes
for a special seal that will be marked "Proof of Purchase Seal."

The last line of the listing indicates whether or not
a refund form is required. At the lower right of each
listing is the expiration date of the offer. The word
"None" means that there is no expiration date.

Abbreviations

The following are the most common abbreviations
found in the refund listings:

Comb. ....Combination. Often used to indicate
that proofs from a combination of sev-
eral different products will be accept-
able.

Cpn. ....Coupon. Usually refers to a manufacturer's cashoff coupon, also called a
cents-off coupon, sometimes abbrevi-
ated as c/o.

Ingred. ....Ingredient.

NFN ....No Form Necessary. Indicates a manufacturer will accept proofs of purchase
without a refund form.

None ....Used to indicate that the offer has no
expiration date.

Nt. Wt. ....Net Weight. Often used to indicate
that a net weight statement is the re-
quired proof of purchase.

P/H ....Postage and Handling. When a manufacturer charges a postage and handling fee, often found on gift refunds.

Pkg. ....Package.

POP ....Proof of Purchase. The label, boxtop, or other part of the package that is requested by the manufacturer for the refund, sometimes called a "Qualifier."

POP Seal ....A special seal usually imprinted on the package. Its sole purpose is to provide the consumer with an easily recognizable proof of purchase.

PP ....Purchase Price. Often used to indicate that you will receive a refund of your purchase price.

Regis. Tape ....Register Tape. The supermarket cash register tape required by many manufacturers as a part of the required proofs of purchase. In most such cases the purchase price of the product must be circled on the tape.

SMP ....Specially Marked Package. Often used to refer to a proof of purchase which can only be found on a specially marked package. The special markings are usually boldly presented on the front of the package.

Stmt. ....Statement. A part of the printed matter on a package, such as the net weight statement, the ingredient statement, or the nutrition information statement.

UPC ....Universal Product Code. The narrow black lines with the numbers below them. Often referred to as the UPC code or symbol.

WSL ....While Supply Lasts. Often used to indicate that a gift offer will end when the supply is exhausted.

21

Refund Offers

FILE NO. 1
Cereals, Breakfast
Products, Baby Products

_____BEECH-NUT, P.O. Box 548, Dept. 36, Canajoharie, NY 13317 (Receive $1 in coupons towards next purchase) Send 5 boxtops from any variety of Beech-Nut Cera-Meal. No form necessary.   12/31/80

_____BRAN CHEX OFFER, P.O. Box PL-14068, Belleville, IL 62222 (Receive free packages of Bran Chex) Send one boxtop from either Bran Buds, All-Bran, 40% Bran Flakes, Cracklin Bran, 100% Bran Flakes or Raisin Bran. No form necessary.   1/31/81

_____1980 CHEX CALENDAR OF CREATIVE COOKING, P.O. Box 9033, St. Paul, MN 55190 (Receive one 1980 Calendar, 24 recipe cards and $4.05 worth of cashoff coupons for various products) Send 8 Chex cereal proof of purchase seals OR $1.50 plus 1 proof of purchase seal. No form necessary.   6/30/80

_____HEINZ BABY FOOD REFUND, P.O. Box 28-D 22, Pittsburgh, PA 15230 (Receive $1 refund) Send 25 labels from Heinz Regular Junior Food jars. Refund form required. 12/31/80

_____HUGGIES DIAPER REBATE OFFER, Box 551-H11, Neenah, WI 54956 (Receive $3 in coupons towards next purchase) Send UPC symbols from any 8 full size Kleenex Huggies Disposable Diaper packages. Refund form required. 12/31/80

_____(KELLOGG'S) BIG YEL-LA TUBE SOCKS OFFER, P.O. Box 9112, St. Paul MN 55191 (Receive a free pair of Big Yella Tube Socks) Send 5 proof of purchase seals from Kellogg's Sugar Corn Pops OR 2 POP seals and 75¢.
No form necessary.   6/30/80

_____(KELLOGG'S) FREE SLIDING PUZZLE OFFER, P.O. Box 2672, Reidsville, NC 27322 (Receive free Kellogg's character sliding puzzle) Send proof of purchase seals from 3 packages of Kellogg's Sugar Smacks cereal for each puzzle. Select character: Dig 'em, Tony the Tiger, Snap! Crackle! Pop!, or Toucan Sam.
No form necessary.   6/30/80

_____(KELLOGG'S) BACK TO SCHOOL BIC PEN OFFER, P.O. Box 9378, St. Paul, MN 55193 (Receive four Bic Ballpoint Pens free) Send 3 proof of purchase seals from Kellogg's Sugar Frosted Flakes cereal.
No form necessary.   8/31/80

_____(KELLOGG'S) FOLEY KITCHEN UTENSILS OFFER, P.O. Box 9125, St. Paul MN 55191 (Receive free Foley Nylon Kitchen Utensils) Send 3 proof of purchase seals from Kellogg's Cracklin' Bran cereal.
No form necessary.   8/31/80

_____KELLOGG'S FRUIT 'N CEREAL OFFER, P.O. Box 9471, St. Paul, MN 55194 (Receive $1 coupon for next purchase of any fresh fruit or cereal) Send 4 proof of purchase seals from any combination of Kellogg's Corn Flakes, Rice Krispies, Sugar Frosted Flakes, or Special K cereals.
No form necessary.   6/30/80

_____(KELLOGG'S) ROCKY II POSTER OFFER, P.O. Box 2690, Reidsville, NC 27322 (Receive a free Rocky poster) Send 3 proof of purchase seals from Kellogg's Graham Crackos cereal.
No form necessary.   8/31/80

_____(KING VITAMIN CEREAL) ERECTOR SET OFFER, P.O. Box 8146, Clinton, IA 52734 (Receive a free Pocket Erector Set) Send 3 purchase seals from King Vitamin Cereal for each set.
Refund form required. 6/30/80

_____KLEENEX DIAPER REBATE OFFER, P.O. Box 551-SD-1, Neenah, WI 54956 (Receive $3 refund or $4 worth of coupons towards next purchase) Send 12 UPC symbols with numbers from any size Kleenex Super Dry disposable diaper cartons.
Refund form required. 12/31/80

_____(POST) COUNTRY TIME OFFER, GENERAL FOODS CORPORATION, P.O. Box 4063 East Court St., Kankakee, IL 60901 (Receive a Country Time 6-pack or a 10-quart Canister) Send 5 boxtops from Post Raisin Bran and/or Post Toasties.
Refund form required. 11/30/80

FREE
COUNTRY TIME
LEMONADE FLAVOR
DRINK OR DRINK MIX
FOR ANY COMBINATION OF
5 BOX TOPS FROM
POST RAISIN BRAN
AND/OR POST TOASTIES
OFFER EXPIRES NOVEMBER 30, 1980
SEE REVERSE SIDE FOR DETAILS

_____(POST) GROW YOUR OWN SALAD OFFER, P.O. Box 6079, Kankakee, IL 60901 (Receive 8 packets Burpee vegetable seeds plus one package Good Seasons Salad Dressing) Send 4 Grow Your Own Salad proof of purchase seals from specially marked packages of Post 40% Bran Flakes.
Refund form required.   6/30/80

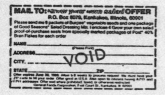

MAIL TO: Grow your own salad OFFER
P.O. Box 6079, Kankakee, Illinois, 60901
Please send me 8 packets of Burpee vegetable seeds and one package of Good Seasons Salad Dressing Mix. I enclose 4 Grow your own salad proof-of-purchase seals from specially marked packages of Post 40% Bran Flakes for each order
NAME
ADDRESS
CITY.
STATE   ZIP

_____(POST GRAPE-NUTS) YOGURT OFFER, P.O. Box 9162, Kankakee, IL 60901 (Receive coupon for three (8-oz. containers of yogurt) Send 4 proof of purchase seals from specially marked packages of Grape-Nuts.
Refund from required.   1/31/81

FILE NO. 2
Dairy Products, Oils, Margarine, Diet Foods

_____BERTOLLI REFUND & FREE COOKBOOK OFFER, P.O. Box 94754, Schaumburg, IL 60194 (Receive 50¢ coupon for next purchase + 32-page recipe book) Send the front paper label from a 17-oz. or larger jar of Bertolli Pure Olive Oil plus register tape with price circled. Note: For tins of oil, write the UPC code number on the cash register tape.
Refund form required.   12/31/80

50¢ Refund & FREE Cookbook Offer
BERTOLLI
Pure Olive Oil
OFFER EXPIRES DECEMBER 31, 1980

_____BORDEN CHEESE 'N FRUIT OFFER, Box 913, Fairfield, CT 06430 (Receive $1.25 refund) Send front labels from any 3 Borden Natural Chunk Cheese packages: Cheddar, Colby, Monterey Jack, Swiss, Mozzarella, Muenster, Blue, Brick, or Provolone, plus register tape showing the price of any fresh fruit or vegetable purchase.
No form necessary.   6/30/80

_____KRAFT BIG CHUNK OF SAVINGS OFFER, P.O. Box 740, Dept. TP, Chicago, IL 60677 (Receive $1 refund) Send 2 labels showing the complete name from any 12-oz. package of Kraft Swiss or Kraft Aged Swiss Cheese.
Refund form required.   6/30/80

_____ORIGINAL HERKIMER COUNTY CHEESE CO., INC. P.O. Box 310, Herkimer, NY 13350 (Receive $1 refund) Send ingredient labels from any 3 packages of Original Herkimer County Cheeses or Cheese Prod.
Refund form required.   6/30/80

_____SLENDER REFUND OF-FER, Box 360, Pico Rivera, CA 90665 (Receive 50¢ refund) Send 1 box bottom from any flavor Slender Diet Meal Bars. Refund form required. 7/31/80

FILE NO. 3
Soups, Snack Foods, Candy

_____APPIAN WAY $1.00 REFUND OFFER, P.O. Box 2363, Maple Plain, MN 55348 (Receive $1 refund) Send 2 Appian Way Pizza weight statements. Refund form required. 6/30/80

_____BUITONI FOODS COR-PORATION, P.O. Box NB-840 El Paso, TX 79977 (Receive 50¢ refund) Send the net weight statements from 2 packages Buitoni Pizza. Refund form required 12/31/80

_____(CAMPBELL'S) CHUN-KY SOUP, Dept. G, P.O. Box 2659, Maple Plain, MN 55348 (Receive $1 refund) Send 5 different 19-oz. Chunky Soup labels or any 8 Single Serving Chunky Soup labels. Refund form required. 6/30/80

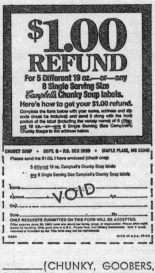

_____(CHUNKY, GOOBERS, RAISINETS, OH HENRY, BIT-O-HONEY) FREE SCHOOL SUPPLIES OFFER, P.O. Box 751,

Young America, MN 55399 (Receive $1 coupon for School Supplies) Send 5 proof of purchase seals from any of the four-paks, or bags for these products.
No form necessary.   6/30/80

————CHUNKY JADE "SWEETHEART" OFFER, P.O. Box 33, Brooklyn, NY 11232 (Free jade "Sweetheart" Necklace) Send 5 "It's Thicker" seals from front panels of any variety of 4- or 6-oz. bars.
No form necessary.   12/30/80

————FRITOS/LIPTON $1.00 REFUND, P.O. Box 8160, Clinton, IA 52736 (Receive $1 refund) Send 2 front panels from boxes of Lipton Onion Recipe and Soup Mix plus 2 net weight statements from 8½-oz. or larger Fritos Brand Corn Chips plus register tape with price circled for any sour cream purchase.
Refund form required. 7/31/80

————FREE LA CHOY LUNCH IN A CUP OFFER, Box NB 308, El Paso, TX 79977 (Receive free package of La Choy Lunch in a Cup) Send the complete ingredient statement from any variety of La Choy Lunch in a Cup.
Refund form required. 6/30/80

————LA PIZZERIA, P.O. Box 1350, Watertown, MA 02172 (Receive $1 refund) Send UPC symbols from 3 packages of La Pizzeria.

Refund form required. 10/31/80

————(RAISINETS, GOOBERS, SNO-CAPS) MOVIE MONEY OFFER, P.O. Box 515, Young America, MN 55399 (Receive $1 refund) Send the yellow "½ pound" burst from two 8-oz. boxes of Raisinets, Goobers, or Sno-Caps.
No form necessary.   12/31/80

————HOMEMADE SOUP STARTER REFUND OFFER, P.O. Box 1140, Arlington Heights, IL 60006 (Receive free package of Soup Starter) Send the word "Stock" cut from stock packet from 2 packages of Soup Starter.
Refund form required. 8/31/80

————STOUFFER'S PIZZA REFUND, P.O. Box 1180, Arlington Heights, IL 60006 (Receive $1 refund) Send three colored Flavor Flags (top right hand corner of package) from any three packages of Stouffer's French Bread Pizzas.
Refund form required 12/31/80

————TEASER POPS $1.00 REFUND, P.O. Box 4447, Chicago, IL 60677 (Receive $1 refund) Send 2 empty bags from Teaser Pops.
No form necessary.   7/1/80

————WHOPPERS ICE CREAM OFFER, P.O. Box NB-875, El Paso, TX 79977 (Receive $1 refund) Send word "Whoppers" from two 8-oz. bags or five 20¢-bags plus brand name panel from one pint or larger size ice cream, any brand. No form necessary. 12/31/80

_____NESTLE, P.O. Box 2057, Maple Plain, MN 55348 (Receive a free Star Wars pendant) Send 10 complete wrappers from Nestle Single Bars (no miniatures). Select character: R2D2, C3PO, Darth Vader, Chewbacca. No form necessary. 11/30/80

FILE NO. 4
Vegetables, Starches, Fruits

_____BIRDS EYE, P.O. Box 9126, Kankakee, IL 60901 (Receive $1 refund) Send tear strips from 5 Birds Eye Cheese Sauce Vegetables. Refund form required. 6/30/80

_____BIRDS EYE, P.O. Box 5217, Kankakee, IL 60901 (Receive 50¢ refund) Send 3 tear strips from Birds Eye Americana Recipe Vegetables. Refund form required. 6/30/80

_____BIRDS EYE, P.O. Box 5002, Kankakee, IL 60901 (Receive 50¢ refund + 40¢ in coupons towards next purchase) Send side tear strips from any 5 Birds Eye American Recipe Vegetables. Refund form required. 6/30/80

_____BIRDS EYE, P.O. Box 3127, Kankakee, IL 60901 (Receive 50¢ refund) Send 3 tear

strips from Birds Eye Combination Vegetables. Refund form required. 6/30/80

_____BUITONI FOODS CORPORATION, P.O. Box NB-119, El Paso, TX 79977 (Receive 50¢ in coupons towards next purchase) Send complete front panel from 2 packages Buitoni Large Round Cheese Ravioli. Refund form required. 12/31/80

_____BUITONI FOODS CORPORATION, P.O. Box NB 842, El Paso, TX 79977. (Free package of Buitoni Spaghetti or Macaroni) Send bursts with word "Light" from front panels of any 3 packages Buitoni High Protein Spaghetti or Macaroni. Refund form required. 12/31/80

_____(BUSH'S) ADVENTURE IN EATING, BUSH BROTHERS & COMPANY, Broadway & Locust Streets, Blytheville, AR 72315 (Receive $1 refund) Send 4 Bush's Best Baked Bean labels 21-oz. size or 8 labels from 9½-oz. size. Refund form required. 6/30/80

_____(BUSH'S) SHOWBOAT PORK & BEANS, Bush Brothers

& Co., Dandridge, TN 37725 (Receive $1 refund) Send 8 labels from Bush's Showboat Pork & Beans.
Refund form required. 6/30/80

_____GREEN GIANT COMPANY, Box 33-525, Le Sueur, MN 56068 (Receive free package of Green Giant Nibblers Corn) Send ingredient panel from 1 package Green Giant 4-ear Niblet Corn-on-the-Cob.
Refund form required. 6/30/80

_____GREEN GIANT COMPANY, Box 16-509, Le Sueur, MN 56058 (Receive free can of Corn) Send ingredient panels from two 12-oz. cans of Green Giant White Corn or Mexicorn.
Refund form required. 6/30/80

_____GREEN GIANT COMPANY, Box 15-536, Le Sueur, MN 56058 (Receive free can of 3-Bean Salad) Send ingredient panels from 2 cans of Green Giant 3-Bean Salad.
Refund form required. 8/31/80

_____MINUTE RICE, P.O. Box 9072, Kankakee, IL 60901 (Receive $1 refund) Send 4 box tops from 14-oz. Minute Rice.
Refund form required. 10/31/80

_____MONTINI, P.O. Box 1210, Arlington Heights, IL 60006 (Receive 40¢ worth of coupons plus Great Tomato Recipes brochure) Send 2 labels from Montini Crushed Tomatoes or Whole Tomatoes.
No form necessary. 8/30/80

_____SUCCESS REFUND, P.O. Box 55259, Houston, TX 77055 (Receive $1 refund) Send 4 proof of purchase seals from any 7-, 14-, or 21-oz. size Success Rice.
Refund form required. 6/30/80

_____(UNCLE BEN'S) HAM & RICE, P.O. Box 1964, Maple Plain, MN 55348. (Receive $1.50 refund) Send 2 proof of purchase seals from Uncle Ben's Wild Rice products plus Golden Star cut from certificate found enclosed in each Golden Star Ham by Armour.
Refund form required. 6/30/80

FILE NO. 5
Seasonings, Sauces, Sugar, Syrup, Salad Dressings

_____BUITONI FOODS CORPORATION, P.O. Box NB-204, El Paso, TX 79977 (Receive free jar of Buitoni Spaghetti Sauce) Send the labels from three 15-oz.

jars or two 29-oz. jars of Buitoni's Spaghetti Sauce.
Refund form required. 12/31/80

_____DURKEE FAMOUS FOODS, 900 Union Commerce Bldg., Cleveland, OH 44155 (Receive 35¢ refund) Send front label from 5-oz. Mr. Mustard.
Refund form required. 12/31/80

_____(EHLERS SAUCE & GRAVY MIXES) EHLERS DIVISION OF BROOKE BOND FOODS, INC., Dept. G, 2 Nevada Drive, Lake Success, NY 11040 (Receive $1 refund) Send the front panels from any 5 Ehlers Sauce & Gravy Mixes.
No form necessary. 6/30/80

_____FAMILY KITCHEN GRAVY OFFER, P.O. Box 1070, Arlington Heights, IL 60006 (Receive free package of Family Kitchen Gravy) Send one proof of purchase symbol from back of any package of Family Kitchen Gravy.
Refund form required. 6/30/80

_____R.T. FRENCH COMPANY, P.O. Box 743, Rochester, NY 14603 (Receive 50¢ refund) Send top half of a Sloppy Hot Dogs package plus one front wrapper from any brand hot dogs.
No form necessary. 12/31/80

_____GOLDEN GRIDDLE OFFER, P.O. Box 5443, Hicksville, NY 11816 (Receive $1 refund) Send 3 front labels from

any size or sizes of Golden Griddle syrup.
Refund form required. 6/30/80

_____MCCORMICK & COMPANY, INC., P.O. Box 1411, Baltimore, MD 21203. (Receive $1.25 refund) Send 3 complete front panels from McCormick Bag 'n Season for chicken or Season 'n Fry for chicken.
No form necessary. 12/31/80

_____MCCORMICK & COMPANY, INC., P.O. Box 1411, Baltimore, MD 21203. (Receive free package of McCormick Season 'n Fry) Send one complete front panel from McCormick Season 'n Fry.
No form necessary. 12/31/80

_____MCCORMICK & COMPANY, INC., P.O. Box 1411, Baltimore, MD 21203 (Receive free package of McCormick

Spaghetti Sauce Mix) Send one complete front panel from economy size package McCormick Spaghetti Sauce Mix.
No form necessary.   12/31/82

_____MCCORMICK/SCHILLING IMITATION VANILLA, P.O. Box NB-709, El Paso, TX 79977 (Receive refund of 75¢ or $1.25) Send complete front label from 2-oz. carton of either McCormick or Schilling's Imitation Vanilla for 75¢ or send label from 4-oz. size for $1.25.
No form necessary.   11/30/80

_____RAGU FOODS, INC., P.O. Box 8186, Clinton IA 52736 (Receive 50¢ coupon towards next purchase) Send labels from any two different styles of 40-oz. size Extra Thick and Zesty, or Classic Combinations or regular Spaghetti Sauce.
No form necessary.   6/30/80

_____SPATINI SPAGHETTI SAUCE, P.O. Box 9231, Clinton IA 52732 (Receive $1 refund) Send 2 name panels from the fronts of 2 cartons of Spatini Spaghetti Sauce Mix plus the price and net weight label from one package of chicken.
Refund form required.   6/30/80

_____WISH-BONE, P.O. Box 8193, Clinton, IA 52736 (Receive free salad dressing bottle) Send neckbands from one Wish-Bone Italian with Cheese Dressing plus one neckband from any other Wish-Bone Italian variety.
No form necessary.   12/31/80

FILE NO. 6
Meat, Poultry, Seafood, Other Main Dishes

_____(ARMOUR) CORNED BEEF HASH REFUND OFFER, P.O. Box 9008, St. Paul, MN 55190 (Receive $1 refund) Send two complete labels from Armour Star hash and word "eggs" from any carton.
Refund form required.   6/30/80

_____(ARMOUR) POTTED MEAT REFUND OFFER, P.O. Box 9166, St. Paul, MN 55191 (Receive $1 refund) Send 9 labels from Armour Star Potted Meat, either size, or 6 labels from 5½-oz. size plus end flap from box of crackers.
Refund form required.   6/30/80

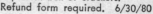

_____(ARMOUR) TREET REFUND OFFER, P.O. Box 9815, St. Paul, MN 55198 (Receive $1 refund) Send 2 front labels from Armour Treet plus end wrapper from any loaf of bread.
Refund form required.   6/30/80

_____(ARMOUR) VIENNA SAUSAGE REFUND OFFER,

P.O. Box 9412, St. Paul MN 55194 (Receive $1 refund) Send 6 labels from any size Armour Vienna Sausage plus word "chip" from any bag of chips.
Refund form required. 6/30/80

_____BUITONI FOODS CORPORATION, P.O. Box NB 837, El Paso, TX 79977 (Receive 50¢ coupon for next purchase) Send complete front panel from 2 packages Buitoni Italian Casseroles or Dinners.
Refund form required. 6/30/80

_____BUITONI FOODS CORPORATION, P.O. Box NB-773, El Paso, TX 79977 (Receive 50¢ coupon for next purchase) Send net weight statements from 2 packages Buitoni Deluxe Entrees/2 compartment dinners.
Refund form required. 12/31/80

_____BUITONI FOODS CORPORATION, P.O. Box NB-119, El Paso, TX 79977 (Receive 50¢ coupon for next purchase) Send front panel from 2 packages of Buitoni Large Round Cheese Ravioli.
Refund form required. 12/31/80

_____HUNTER HOT DOG OFFER, P.O. Box NB-871, El Paso, TX 79977 (Receive free pound of Hunter Hot Dogs) Send complete package front from either Hunter Jumbo Hot Dogs or Beef Dinner Franks package.

Refund form required. 12/31/80

_____KREY WIENER OFFER, P.O. Box NB-160, El Paso, TX 79977 (Receive free pound of Krey Wieners) Send the complete package front from one Krey Wiener package. Does not apply to Ball Game Hot Dogs or Gourmet Franks.
Refund form required. 12/31/80

_____LIBBY'S CANNED MEATS OFFER, P.O. Box 7077, Dept. M, Chicago, IL 60677 (Receive $1—$3.50 refund or

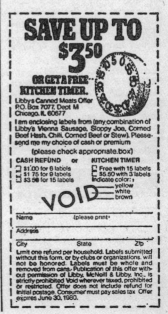

Kitchen Timer) Send labels from any combination of Libby's Vienna Sausage, Sloppy Joe, Corned Beef Hash, Chili, Corned Beef or Stew. Six labels = $1, 9 = $1.75, 15 = $3.50 OR send 15 labels and select a kitchen timer, OR 3 labels + $5.50 for timer. Select timer in yellow, white, or brown.
Refund form required.　6/30/80

_____(MRS. PAUL'S) SUPREME LIGHT BATTER COUPON OFFER, Mrs. Paul's Kitchens, Inc., P.O. Box 5835, Philadelphia, PA 19128 (Receive $1 coupon for future purchase of Supreme Light Batter products plus your postage costs) Send the "Satisfaction Guarantee" panel from Mrs. Paul's Supreme Light Batter products as follows: 4 Supreme Light Batter Fish Fillets (2 pack) OR 2 Supreme Light Batter Fish Fillets (5 pack) OR 3 Supreme Light Batter Fish Kabobs.
Refund form required. 6/30/80

_____RUPERT'S CERTI-FRESH, P.O. Box 1080, West Covina, CA 91793 (Receive $1–$4 refund) Send ingredient flaps from Certi-Fresh Batter Fried Shrimp, Fish 'N Chips, Sole in Butter Sauce, Batter Fried Fish Sticks or Batter Fried Cod; 2 different flaps = $1, 3 different = $2, 4 different = $3, all 5 different = $5.
Refund form required. 12/31/80

_____SEAPAK REFUND OFFER, P.O. Box NB-776, El Paso, TX 79977 (Receive $1–$2.50 refund) Send ingredient statements from 2 SeaPak seafood products for $1. Send 5 for $2.50. Proof of purchase must be from at least 2 different Sea-Pak products.

Refund form required.　6/30/80

_____STOUFFER'S, P.O. Box NB-716, El Paso, TX 79977 (Receive 50¢–$1 refund) Send name and weight portion from front of carton of any Stouffer's International Entrees: Chicken Paprikash, Swedish Meatballs, Linguini, Beef Teriyaki, Beef Chop Suey, Chicken Cacciatore. One = 50¢, 2 = $1.
Refund form required.　6/80

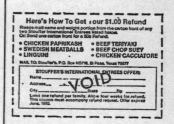

_____STOUFFER'S CREPES, P.O. Box 1200, Arlington Heights, IL 60006 (Receive $1 refund) Send UPC symbol with number from 2 packages of Stouffer's Crepes.
Refund form required. 1/1/81

_____STOUFFER'S STUFFED SHELLS, Box 1070, Arlington Heights, IL 60006 (Receive 50¢ refund) Send information panels from the back package panel of any 2 Stouffer's Stuffed Shells.
Refund form required. 1/1/81

_____(SWIFT'S WINDOW-SILL PLANTER OFFER, P.O.

Box 406, Downers Grove, IL 60515 (Receive two planters of Rainbow Coleus and Ornamental Peppers) Send two ingredient end flaps from any Swift Premium International Entree packages.
Refund form required. 6/30/80

FILE NO. 7
Baked Goods, Desserts

_____(FLAKO PIE CRUST MIX) FLAKO FILLING REFUND, P.O. Box 2716, Maple Plain, MN 55348 (Receive refund for purchase price of pie filling) Send proofs of purchase from **two** packages of Flako Pie Crust Mix, and from **one** can of pie filling, plus cash register receipt with filling price circled. Exact type of proofs not specified.
Refund form required. 6/30/80

_____(JELLO, DREAM WHIP, COOL WHIP, BAKER'S) CASH OR COUPONS REFUND, GENERAL FOODS CORP., P.O. Box 3151, East Court St., Kankakee, IL 60901 (Receive $1–$2 refund) Make at least 2 pies. Clip the UPC code from 2 of the following ingredients: Jello Brand Gelatin and Cool Whip Topping, Jello Brand Pudding and Dream Whip Topping, Cool Whip Topping and Baker's Coconut, or Baker's Coconut and Baker's Chocolate. Refund form required.

_____JELLO CHEESECAKE CASH REFUND, P.O. Box 4177 Kankakee, IL 60901 (Receive 75¢ refund) Send 3 Jello cheesecake box tops.
Refund form required. 9/1/80

_____MARTHA WHITE FOODS, INC. P.O. 55255 Houston TX 77055 (Receive $1 refund) Send the boxtops or front pouch panels from any 4 Martha White Mixes or Gladiola Mixes. No form necessary. 7/31/80

_____(NORWEGIAN IDEAL FLATBREAD) IDEAL REFUND, P.O. Box 2158, Glenbrook, CT 06906 (Receive 30¢ or $1 refund) Send net weight statements from any packages of Ideal Flatbread as follows: 1 statement = 30¢, 3 statements = $1.
Refund form required. 12/31/80

_____ROYAL DESSERTS OFFER, P.O. Box 7025, Westbury, NY 11592 (Receive free package of Royal Pudding) Send front panels from any 3 Royal Pudding packages.
Refund form required. 9/30/80

_____SALERNO-MEGOWEN BISCUIT CO., P.O. Box NB-299, El Paso, TX 79977 (Receive $1 refund) Send proof of purchase seals or UPC symbols from 4 different Salerno products.
No form necessary. 10/1/80

_____SUNSHINE FREE FILM OFFER, Dept. 086, P.O. Box 7620, Philadelphia, PA. 19101 (Receive a free roll of film plus 20¢ worth of coupons) Send 60¢

for postage and handling plus one proof of purchase seal from any size Hydrox, Vanilla Wafers, Vienna Fingers, or Oatmeal Peanut cookies. Be sure to specify 110 or 126 film.
Refund form required. 6/30/80

_____(WASA CRISP BREAD) WASA, P.O. Box 2160-F, Glenbrook, CT 06906 (Receive $1 refund) Send the net weight statements from any 3 packages of Wasa Crisp Bread.
Refund form required. 12/31/80

FILE NO. 8
Beverages

_____COUNTRY TIME OFFER, P.O. Box 3120, Kankakee, IL 60901 (Receive a free package of Country Time Lemonade) Send 5 "Country Time Offer" Proof of Purchase seals.
Refund form required. 11/30/80

_____FREE LIPTON TEA BALL OFFER, P.O. Box 8550, Clinton, IA 52732 (Receive a one- or six-cup Tea Ball) Send the entire box top with the Lipton name and net weight from 2 boxes of Lipton 8-oz. loose tea. State tea ball size selection.

Refund form required. 12/31/80

_____MAXIM GREAT BREAKFAST RECIPE COLLECTION, P.O. Box 7025, Kankakee, IL 60901 (Receive free recipes on 4" x 6" cards) Send one inner seal from any size jar of Maxim Freeze-dried Coffee.
Refund form required. 6/30/80

_____(MAXWELL HOUSE) PARTIES TO REMEMBER BOOKLET OFFER, General Foods Corporation, P.O. Box 2003, Kankakee, IL 60901 (Receive a free booklet, Party Ideas, Tips, Coffee Serving Tips) Send one inner seal from any 6-, 10-, or 14-oz. jar of Maxwell House Instant Coffee.
Refund form required. 6/30/80

_____FREE MILK MATE OFFER, P.O. Box 3000, Winston-Salem NC 27102 (Receive a free 1/2 gallon of milk, value up to $1.25) Send the net weight statements removed from either 3 bottles of 20-oz. Milk Mate or 2 bottles of 36-oz.
Refund form required. 12/31/80

_____NESTLÉ, P.O. Box 1223, Boston, MA 02172 (Receive 50¢ coupon for you and 20¢ coupons for 2 neighbors towards next purchase) Send names and addresses of 2 neighbors as well as your own.
Refund form required. 12/31/80

_____ORANGE PLUS REFUND, General Foods Corporation, P.O. Box 3029, East Court St., Kankakee, IL 60901 (Receive five 20¢-coupons towards next purchase of Orange Plus OR 50¢ refund) Send the opening tear strip from one 12-oz. or 16-oz. can; OR the tear strip from two 6-oz. cans of Orange Plus and send the UPC number from

each can and the mail-in certificate checked "I agree" for $1 worth of coupons OR "I disagree" for 50¢ refund.
Refund form required. 6/30/80

_____OVALTINE, P.O. Box 4447, Chicago, IL 60677 (Receive $1 refund) Send 3 Ovaltine labels, chocolate or malt.
Refund form required. 6/30/80

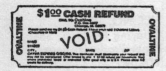

_____SANKA BRAND DECAFFEINATED COFFEE, P.O. Box 6088, Kankakee, IL 60901 (Receive $1 refund) Send 12 empty Sanka Brand Decaffeinated Coffee envelopes, freeze-dried or instant.
Refund form required. 6/30/80

_____SWISS MISS SKI PATCH OFFER, P.O. Box 9017, St. Paul, MN 55190 (Receive 3-color embroidered U.S. Ski Team Patch) Send 25¢ postage and handling plus U.S. Ski Team symbol from any carton or canister of Swiss Miss Hot Cocoa Mix.
No form necessary. 12/31/80

_____(TETLEY) FREE FILM OFFER, C/O TPL, Dept. 325, P.O. Box 7620, Philadelphia PA 19101 (Receive free color film plus a 20¢ coupon) Send 60¢ for postage and handling plus one label from any package of

Tetley Iced Tea Mix or Instant Tea. Specify either 110 or 126 film.
Refund form required. 6/30/80

_____WAGNER TIC TAC TOE REFUND, P.O. Box 1056, Tinley Park IL 60477 (Receive $1 refund) Refund form required.

CHECK YOUR
TIC TAC TOE LABEL COMBINATION

ACROSS
☐ PEACH, TROPICAL PUNCH, GRAPE
☐ GRAPEFRUIT, ORANGE, APPLE
☐ APPLE, ORANGE-PINEAPPLE, GRAPEFRUIT

DOWN
☐ PEACH, APPLE-FRUIT, APPLE
☐ TROPICAL PUNCH, ORANGE, ORANGE-PINEAPPLE
☐ GRAPE, APPLE, GRAPEFRUIT

DIAGONALLY
☐ PEACH, ORANGE, GRAPEFRUIT
☐ APPLE, ORANGE, GRAPE

FILE NO. 9
Miscellaneous Food Products

_____ADOLPH'S MEAT DEPT. OFFER, P.O. Box 9159, Clinton, IA 52736 (Receive $1 coupon towards next meat purchase) Send the large red panels on the front of the packages from: any 3 Adolph's Marinade in Minutes—Barbecue, Garlic, Steak Sauce or Italian Herb; Firm & Moist Meatloaf Mix; 1 Hour Stew Mix; PLUS price stickers from $3 or more of any meat, plus name and address of store where purchased.
No form necessary. 6/30/80

_____BAKER'S OFFER, General Foods Corp., P.O. Box 2027, East Court St., Kankakee, IL 60901 (Receive four 25¢-cou-

pons towards next purchase)
Send two front panels from any
size of the following packages:
Baker's Coconut; Baker's German Sweet Chocolate; Baker's
Semi-Sweet Chocolate; or Baker's Unsweetened Chocolate.
Refund form required. 12/31/80

_____JIF CHOOSY MOTHER'S PEANUT BUTTER COOKBOOK OFFER, P.O. Box 284,
Maple Plain, MN 55348 (Receive a free cookbook) Send
50¢ for postage and handling
plus the net weight statement
from one jar any size JIF Peanut Butter.
Refund form required. 8/1/80

_____OVEN FRY REFUND
OFFER, P.O. Box 6057, Kankakee, IL 60901 (Receive 50¢ refund) Send 3 direction panels
from any size or recipe of Oven
Fry Coating Mix for Chicken.
Refund form required. 9/30/80

_____(REGINA VINEGAR)
HEUBLEIN, INC., P.O. Box 821,
Meriden, CT 06450 (Receive
35¢ refund) Send the sprinkle
spout from top of one Regina
Wine Vinegar bottle.
Refund form required. 9/30/81

_____SKIPPY OFFER, P.O.
Box 307-SOF, Dept. E, Coventry,
CT 06238 (Receive full purchase
price refund) Send part of label
with words "Naturally Just Peanuts and Salt" plus register tape
with price circled from Skippy

Old Fashioned Peanut Butter.
Refund form required. 6/30/80

_____SKIPPY PEANUT BUTTER OFFER, P.O. Box 5285,
Hicksville, NY 11816 (Receive
$2 refund) Send the net weight
statements from four 40-oz. jars
of Skippy Creamy or Super
Chunk.
Refund form required. 6/30/80

_____STEWART SANDWICHES, P.O. Box NB-914, El
Paso, TX 79977 (Receive $1 refund) Send 3 heating instruction
panels from any Stewart Sandwich packages.
Refund form required. 12/31/80

FILE NO. 10
Cleaning Products, Soap, Paper Products, Bags, Wraps

_____ALL 10% REFUND
OFFER, P.O. Box NB-764, El
Paso, TX 79977 (Receive a refund of 10% of your store purchases up to $3) Send register
tape and circle total amount of
your purchases and circle at
least 2 ALL purchases plus 4
proofs of purchase from at least
2 ALL brands. The proof of purchase from Concentrated and
Dishwasher ALL is the net
weight statement cut from front
panel of any size box. Proof of
purchase from Liquid ALL is the
net weight statement cut from
front label of any size bottle.
Refund form required. 12/31/80

_____AUTOMATIC VANISH
SOLID 50¢ REFUND, P.O. Box
14164, Baltimore, MD 21268
(Receive 50¢ refund) Send neckband plus register tape with
price circled of Automatic Vanish Solid.
Refund form required. 6/30/80

_____BAGGIES FREE RIBBED SANDWICH OFFER, P.O. Box 594, Young America, MN 55399 (Receive a free package of Baggies Sandwich Bags) Send words "Colgate-Palmolive Co." from any size box of Baggies Food Storage or Sandwich Bags. Refund form required. 6/30/80

_____BOLT $1.00 CASH REFUND OFFER, P.O. Box 9150, Kankakee, IL 60901 (Receive $1 refund) Send the word "Bolt" from the front of 3 Bolt Paper Towel packages.
Refund form required. 6/30/80

_____BRAWNY FREE PACKAGE OFFER, P.O. Box 2668, Maple Plain, MN 55348 (Receive free package of Brawny Towels) Send the pictures of two Brawny Lumberjacks from packages of Brawny Towels.
Refund form required. 7/31/80

_____CRYSTAL WHITE— "GET ONE FREE OFFER", P.O. Box 553, Young America, MN 55399 (Receive a free bottle of Crystal White Dish Liquid) Send the register tape with purchase prices of two bottles of Crystal White Dish Liquid circled and the UPC number written on the tape.

Refund form required. 6/30/80

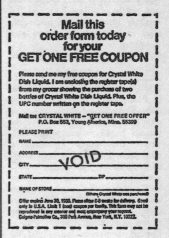

Mail this
order form today
for your
GET ONE FREE COUPON

Please send me my free coupon for Crystal White Dish Liquid. I am enclosing the register tape(s) from my grocer showing the purchase of two bottles of Crystal White Dish Liquid. Plus, the UPC number written on the register tape.

Mail to: CRYSTAL WHITE — "GET ONE FREE OFFER"
P.O. Box 553, Young America, Minn. 55399

PLEASE PRINT

NAME_____

ADDRESS_____

CITY_____

STATE_____ ZIP

NAME OF STORE_____
(Where Crystal White was purchased)

Offer expires June 30, 1980. Please allow 6-8 weeks for delivery. Good only in U.S.A. Limit 1 (one) coupon per family. This form may not be reproduced in any manner and must accompany your request. Colgate-Palmolive Co., 300 Park Avenue, New York, N.Y. 10022.

_____FINAL TOUCH $1.00 REFUND OFFER, P.O. Box NB-346, El Paso, TX 79977 (Receive $1.15 refund) Send one fluid ounce statement cut from the label of any size Final Touch. Refund form required. 12/30/80

_____(GLAD) LARGE KITCHEN GARBAGE BAG HOLDER, P.O. Box 9251, St. Paul, MN 55192 (Receive a free garbage bag holder) Send three UPC codes from 3 boxes of any size Glad Large Kitchen Garbage Bags.
Refund form required. 12/31/80

_____"GLAD" LEAF BAG CADDY, P.O. Box 9226, St. Paul, MN 55192 (Receive a free Leaf Bag Caddy) Send UPC codes from 2 boxes of any Glad Lawn Clean-up Bags.
Refund form required. 12/31/80

_____(GLASS PLUS) SCOTTS INTERNATIONAL, 1300 Highway 8, St. Paul, MN 55412 (Re-

ceive a free Ray-O-Vac Flashlight) Send the UPC code from one bottle of Glass Plus and the register tape with the price circled and 30¢ for postage and handling.
Refund form required. 10/31/80

_____HANDI-BAG $2.00 REFUND OFFER, P.O. Box 7803, El Paso, TX 79975 (Receive an immediate $2 refund in the mail plus a Bounce Back refund form for up to $5 refund with additional purchases) Purchase a minimum of $3.95 worth of Handi-Bag items. Send the UPC symbols, or item numbers if no UPCs, plus the register tape with the Handi-Bag items circled. Indicate name of store where purchased.
Refund form required. 12/31/80

_____K2r STAIN DIAL AND COUPON OFFER, P.O. Box 2933, Maple Plain, MN 55348 (Receive a K2r Stain Dial and a 50¢ coupon) Send in the certificate from a specially marked package of K2r.
Refund form required. 6/30/80

_____KORDITE 10% OFFER, P.O. Box 9142, Clinton, IA 52736 (Receive a 10% refund up to $3) Send 5 premium seals from any Kordite products plus the store cash register receipt showing total purchases. Receive

10% of the total up to $3.00.
Refund form required. 6/30/80

_____KORDITE TURKEY OFFER, Box 9214, Clinton, IA 52736 (Receive a $2 coupon towards the purchase of a turkey) Send 4 premium seals from any Kordite products.
Refund form required. 6/30/80

_____LIQUID ALL $1.00 REFUND OFFER, P.O. Box 9766, St. Paul, MN 55197 (Receive $1.15 refund) Send the fluid ounce statement cut from one label of any size Liquid All.
Refund form required. 12/31/80

_____MARCAL HANKIE OFFER, P.O. Box 120, Elmwood Park, NJ 07407 (Receive 3 free packages of Marcal Hankies) Send the lids from 6 boxes of Marcal Hankies.
No form necessary. 6/30/80

_____MARCAL FACIAL TISSUE OFFER, P.O. Box 1505, Elmwood Park, NJ 07407 (Receive a free box of Marcal Facial Tissues) Send the quality seals from 3 boxes of Marcal Fluff Out 200-count Facial Tissues.
No form necessary. 12/31/80

_____MARCAL HANKIE OFFER, P.O. Box 1506, Elmwood Park, NJ 07407 (Receive a free box of Marcal Hankies) Send 3 quality seals from Marcal Hankie boxes.
No form necessary. 12/31/80

_____FREE SCOTTIES OFFER, P.O. Box 4275, Chester, PA

19016 (Receive a free box of Scotties Tissues) Send 4 proofs of purchase from any boxes of Scotties or Scotties Prints. Exact type of proofs not specified.
Refund form required. 9/1/80

_____WALDORF FLYING DISC OFFER, P.O. Box 4235, Chester, PA 19016 (Receive a free flying Disc) Send 5 seals of Value from Waldorf Bath Tissue.
No form necessary. 6/30/80

_____FREE WALDORF LABEL OFFER, P.O. Box 9739, St. Paul, MN 55197 (Receive 1000 free personalized address labels) Send 5 Waldorf Seals of Value or plain Seals from Family Scott Tissues.
No form necessary. 12/31/80

FILE NO. 11
Sect. A
Health Products

_____BONINE 50¢ OFFER REFUND, P.O. Box NB-316, El Paso, TX 79977 (Receive 50¢ refund) Send top of package with words "Prevents Motion Sickness."
Refund form required. 12/1/80

_____FAMILY CHERACOL D REFUND OFFER, P.O. Box NB-703, El Paso, TX 79977 (Receive 65¢ refund) Send one front panel from Family Cheracol D,

4- or 6-oz. carton.
Refund form required. 6/30/80

_____FLINTSTONES MUG OFFER, P.O. Box 2650, Reidsville, NC 27322 (Receive a free Flintstones Drinking Mug) Send the end flap with picture of Fred Flintstone from Flintstones vitamins plus 35¢ for postage and handling. Select from following character mugs: Fred, Bamm Bamm, Pebbles, or Dino.
Refund form required. 3/1/81

_____HALLS FREE BAG OFFER, P.O. Box 9808, St. Paul, MN 55199 (Receive free bag of Halls Cough Tablets) Send 2 empty 30- or 60-count bags of Halls Cough Tablets.
No form necessary. 8/31/80

_____HALLS BAGS $1.00 REFUND OFFER, P.O. Box 9914, St. Paul, MN 55199 (Receive $1 refund) Send any 3 empty Halls 30-tablet bags.
No form necessary. 8/31/80

_____KAOPECTATE REFUND OFFER, P.O. Box NB-054, El Paso, TX 79977 (Receive 50¢ refund) Send the upper lefthand corner of the front label from

Kaopectate or Kaopectate Concentrate, 8- or 12-oz. size package.
Refund form required. 6/30/80

—————LANACANE, P.O. Box NB-303, El Paso, TX 79977 (Receive 75¢ refund) Send code number appearing on bottom of Lanacane Medicane Dry Skin Lotion plus receipt with Dry Skin Lotion price circled.
Refund form required. 6/30/81

—————(LANACANE BATH TREATMENT) LANACANE, P.O. Box NB-201, El Paso, TX 79977 (Receive $1 refund) Send the number shown on the bottom of back label plus a cash register receipt with the Bath Treatment price circled.
Refund form required. 12/31/81

—————METAMUCIL REFUND OFFER, P.O. Box NB-877, El Paso, TX 79977 (Receive 50¢ refund) Send one inner cap seal from Metamucil Powder 7-, 14-, or 21-oz. size, or top panel from Metamucil Instant Mix, pack of 16 or 20.
Refund form required. 6/30/80

—————MURINE REGULAR FORMULA REFUND OFFER,

P.O. Box NB-241, El Paso, TX 79977 (Receive 50¢ refund plus 25¢ coupon towards next purchase) Send one boxtop from any size carton of Murine Regular Formula.
Refund form required. 12/31/80

—————NATURITE HEALTH PRODUCTS, 6330 Chalet Drive, Los Angeles, CA 90040 (Receive 50¢ refund) Send the part of the Naturite label which includes the word "Naturite" and the name of the product.
No form necessary. 12/31/80

—————NOVAHISTINE, One Industrial Drive, P.O. Box 5602, Maple Plain, MN 55348 (Receive the full purchase price up to $1.25 for a bottle of aspirin, any brand) Send the panel with the ingredients from any size box of one Novahistine product: Elixir, Tablets, Sinus Tablets, DMX or Cough Formula plus the price sticker from the aspirin plus a dated cash register receipt with the aspirin price circled.
Refund form required. 6/30/80

—————SINE-OFF EXTRA STRENGTH ASPIRIN FREE REFUND OFFER, P.O. Box NB-063,

El Paso, TX 79977 (Receive 50¢ refund) Send the complete product code symbol from the back panel of one box of Sine-Off Extra Strength.
Refund form required. 12/31/80

_____UNICAP REFUND OFFER, P.O. Box NB-053, El Paso, TX 79977 (Receive $1 refund) Send the ingredient panel from any package of Unicap Vitamins, 60-tablet size or larger, except chewable.
Refund form required. 6/30/80

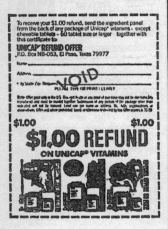

_____UNICAP-T REFUND OFFER, P.O. Box NB-686, El Paso, TX 79977 (Receive $1 refund) Send ingredient panel from one bottle of Unicap-T Vitamins, 90-tablet size or larger.
Refund form required. 6/30/80

_____VAGISIL, P.O. Box 328 A6, White Plains, NY 10604 (Receive 50¢ refund) Send the back panels from one Vagisil carton plus receipt with price circled.
No form necessary. 12/31/80

FILE NO. 11
Sect. B Personal Products

_____BIC SHAVER $1.00 REFUND OFFER, P.O. Box NB-768, El Paso, TX 79977 (Receive $1 refund) Send words "Bic Shaver" from the front of 2 packages.
Refund form required. 12/31/80

_____CEPACOL CASH REFUND OFFER, P.O. Box 2338, Maple Plain, MN 55348 (Receive 50¢ refund) Send the red shoulder label from one 24-oz.-size bottle of Cepacol plus register receipt with price circled.
Refund form required. 6/30/81

_____CEPACOL CASH REFUND OFFER, P.O. Box 4535, Maple Plain, MN 55348 (Receive 40¢ or $1 refund) Send 2 red shoulder labels from 24-oz. Cepacol for $1, or one shoulder label for 40¢ plus cash register receipt with price circled for each refund.
Refund form required. 3/31/81

_____CLOSE-UP LIPSTICK OFFER, P.O. Box 9890, St. Paul,

MN 55198 (Receive a free Max Factor Maxi-Moist Lipstick) Send two back panels with words "Lever Brothers Company" and weight designations from two cartons of Large or Family Size Close-Up Toothpaste, regular or mint, plus 25¢ for postage and handling.

No form necessary.   6/30/80

_____DESITIN SKIN CARE REFUND, Box NB-765, El Paso, TX 79977 (Receive 50¢ refund and 50¢ coupon towards next purchase) Send sticker found on package and write code number found on bottom of Desitin Skin Care Lotion plus cash register receipt with price circled.

Refund form required.   6/30/80

_____ESOTÉRICA,   Dept. 0379-200, Norcliff Thayer, Inc., I Scarsdale Road., Tuckahoe, NY 10707 (Receive $1 refund and two 50¢ coupons) Send blank piece of paper with your name and address with the 7-digit code number found on the back of the Esotérica lotion bottle plus register receipt with price circled.

Refund form required.   6/30/80

_____GENTLE TOUCH $2 REFUND OFFER, I Industrial Drive, P.O. Box 2147, Maple Plain, MN 55348 (Receive $2 refund) Send 6 points worth of proofs of purchase. One point

= net weight statement from front of Gentle Touch Soap package; 3 points = net weight statement from front of Gentle Touch Beads package, or sticker from neck of Gentle Touch Lotion bottle with words "New" or "Contains Baby Oil" plus receipt with price circled for each product.

Refund form required. 12/31/80

_____GILLETTE ATRA RAZOR REBATE OFFER, P.O. Box 9999, St. Paul, MN 55199 (Receive $2 refund) Send one Atra proof of purchase seal from the back of the razor package.

Refund form required. 12/31/80

_____(GILLETTE)   FOAMY TROPICAL COCONUT RE-FUND, P.O. Box 2433, Maple Plain, MN 55348 (Receive 50¢ refund) Send the proof of purchase sticker from bottom of 11-oz. Gillette Foamy Tropical Coconut Shave Cream.

Refund form required. 9/30/80

_____(MENNEN)   SPEED STICK OFFER, P.O. Box 1007, Tinton Falls, NJ 07724 (Receive 50¢ refund and 50¢ coupon) Send refund sticker found on package plus register tape with

price circled and write Mennen Company zip code on tape.
No form necessary.   6/30/80

_____MILK PLUS 6 SHAMPOO REFUND, P.O. Box 2114, Maple Plain, MN 55348 (Receive 75¢ refund) Send a tracing of the words "Milk Plus 6" from the bottle of any formula plus cash register receipt.
No form necessary.   6/30/80

_____MILK PLUS 6 SKIN CARE REFUND OFFER, P.O. Box 2722, Maple Plain, MN 55348 (Receive $1 or $2.50 refund) To receive $1 send words "24 Hour Moisturizer" from one carton of Milk Plus 6 Moisturizer or trace the words "Milk Plus 6" from the jar of Milk Plus 6 Cleanser. In each case send a register receipt with the product price circled. If you send both proofs of purchase, you receive $2.50.
No form necessary.   6/30/80

_____POLIDENT REFUND OFFER, P.O. Box 8911, Clinton, IA 52736 (Receive $1 refund) Send two proof of purchase seals from the bottom panels from any size Polident Tablets, except trial size.

Refund form required. 6/30/81

_____POLIDENT DENTURE CLEANSER REFUND OFFER, P.O. Box 8536, Clinton, IA 52736 (Receive 50¢ refund) Send two boxtops with price spot from any size Polident Tablets Denture Cleanser.
Refund form required. 8/31/80

_____(PRO-TEX HAND CREAM) REFUND OFFER, Box 13621, Philadelphia, PA 19101 (Receive 60¢ refund) Send words "ProTex" from front panel of Pro-Tex protective hand cream plus cash register receipt with price circled.
No form necessary.   12/31/80

_____(SALLY HANSEN) FACIAL HAIR BLEACH REBATE, Sally Hansen Div., Del Laboratories, Inc. Farmingdale, NY 11735 (Receive $1 refund) Send the picture panel from the boxtop of Sally Hansen Facial Hair Bleach.
Refund form required. 6/30/80

FILE NO. 11
Sect. C Cosmetics

_____(REVLON) INSTANT STYLING PERM OFFER, P.O. Box NB-250, El Paso, TX 79977 (Receive $2 refund) Send one boxtop from any formula Revlon-Realistic, new instant Styling Perm.
Refund form required. 6/30/80

FILE NO. 12
Sect. A
Miscellaneous Non-Food Products

_____BATTLESTAR GALAC-

TICA CYLON LEADER OFFER, P.O. Box 813, Hawthorne, CA 90250 (Receive a free toy figure of a Battlestar Galactica character) Send the Battlestar Galactica name from four packages of Mattel's Battlestar Galactica 4-inch figures.
No form necessary.   6/30/80

_____(DUPONT) CAR CARE PRODUCTS REFUND, P.O. Box 43, Ronks, PA 17572 (Receive 50¢ refund) Send entire wrapper from Rally Big Sport Sponge plus register tape or receipt with price circled.
Refund form required. 12/31/81

_____(DUPONT) CAR CARE PRODUCTS REFUND, P.O. Box 43, Ronks, PA 17572 (Receive 75¢ refund) Send CS code number from the back of a can of DuPont Carb and Choke Spray Cleaner plus the register tape with the price circled.
Refund form required. 12/31/81

_____(DUPONT) RALLY REBATE OFFER, P.O. Box 13627, Ronks, PA 17572 (Receive 60¢ refund) Send the "Rally" name from the front of an 8-oz. package of Rally Cream Wax plus the register receipt with price circled.
Refund form required. 12/31/80

_____(GENERAL ELECTRIC LONG LIFE WHITE LIGHT BULBS) GE REBATE OFFER, P.O. Box 2479, Maple Plain, MN 55348 (Receive $1 refund) Send the UPC code and wattage number cut from 2 General Electric 2-bulb Long Life Packages plus the register receipt with the prices circled.
Refund form required. 12/1/80

MAGOOPON

VOID

GE LONG LIFE WHITE LIGHT BULBS
$1.00 REBATE

_____(GENERAL ELECTRIC SOFT WHITE FOUR-PAK LIGHT BULBS) GE REBATE OFFER, P.O. Box 1236, Maple Plain, MN 55348 (Receive $1 refund) Send the UPC code and wattage number cut from a four bulb pack of General Electric Soft White Light Bulbs plus the register receipt with price circled.
Refund form required. 12/1/80

_____JOHNSON'S ODOR-EATERS, P.O. Box NB-209, El Paso, TX 79977 (Receive 50¢ refund) Send back panel from any carton of Odor-Eaters plus register tape with price circled.
Refund form required. 6/30/81

50¢ CASH REFUND On REGULAR OR LEATHER BROWN VOID Odor-Eaters ODOR-DESTROYING COMFORT INSOLES See back for details

_____(ODOR-EATERS) FUNGUS FIGHTERS INSOLES, P.O. Box 328-A7, White Plains,

NY 10604 (Receive 50¢ refund) Send the back panel from one Odor-Eaters Fungus Fighter carton plus register receipt with price circled.
Refund form required. 10/31/80

_____SIMONIZ 75¢ REFUND, P.O. Box 2624, Reidsville, NC 27322 (Receive 75¢ refund) Send the proof of purchase seal from the back label of Liquid Simoniz Car Wax.
Refund form required. 1/1/81

_____TURTLE EXTRA REFUND, P.O. Box NB-975, El Paso, TX 79977 (Receive $2 refund) Send plastic proof of purchase strip from inside Turtle Wax bottle and attach it to sales receipt plus enter "t" number found on the backs of two other Turtle Wax products on collar band containing refund form and include register tape for these two products.
Refund form required. 6/30/80

FILE NO. 12
Section B Pet Products

_____FRISKIES DINNERS MAIL-IN OFFER, Box 590, Pico Rivera, CA 90665 (Receive $1 coupon towards next purchase) Send the top halves of front labels showing brand and variety from 15 cans Friskies Dinners, any size or variety.
Refund form required. 12/31/80

_____MIGHTY DOG CALENDAR OFFER, Box 450-B, Pico Rivera, CA 90665 (Receive free 1980 Calendar) Send 20 complete Mighty Dog dog food labels.
Refund form required. 6/30/80

_____MILK-BONE REFUND, P.O. Box 5000, Westbury, NY 11591 (Receive 25¢—$3 refund) Send completed crossword puzzle in form plus boxtops from any combination of Milk-Bone Brand Dog Biscuits either Original or Beef flavor as follows: 2 boxtops—25¢, 3—50¢, 4—$1, 6—$2, 8—$3.
Refund form required. 6/30/80

_____(9-LIVES CAT FOOD) 1980 MORRIS CALENDAR OFFER, P.O. Box 55195-1, Houston, TX 77055 (Receive free Morris the Cat 1980 Calendar) Send 25 labels from 6-oz. or 6½-oz. cans OR 10 labels from 12-oz. or 13-oz. cans. Also available for $1.25 plus 15 labels from 6-oz. or 6½-oz. OR $1.25 plus 6 labels from 12-oz. or 13-oz.
Refund form required. 6/30/80

_____(PURINA) FIELD 'N FARM REFUND OFFER, P.O. Box PL49, Belleville, IL 62222 (Receive $3 refund or $3.50 in coupons) Send 4 weight triangles from 50 pound Field 'n Farm Dog Meal. State which refund you want; Kansas residents must take coupon.
Refund form required. 6/30/80

_____1980 PURINA CAT CHOW CALENDAR, P.O. Box 2181, Maple Plain, MN 55348 (Receive free 1980 Calendar) Send proof of purchase weight circles from Cat Chow boxes or bags to equal 6 points as follows: 22-oz. box-1 pt., 4-lb. bag-2 pts., 10-lb. bag-4 pts., 20-lb bag-6 pts. Also point from Country Blend or Kitten Chow: 1 pt. for each box; 2 pts. for each bag.
No form necessary.   6/30/80

_____(TENDER   VITTLES) RALSTON PURINA CO., P.O. Box PL35, Belleville, IL 62222 (Receive 3 free boxes of Tender Vittles) Send 9 proof of purchase seals from either nine 6-oz. Tender Vittles boxes, nine 12-oz. boxes, or nine 18-oz. boxes. Don't mix your proofs of purchase.
Refund form required. 6/30/80

_____(TONY DOG FOOD) TONY REWARD, Bush Brothers & Co., Dandridge, TN 37725 (Receive $1 refund) Send 12 pictures of the "Tony Sheriff" from the front label.

Refund form required. 6/30/80

_____(WHISKER   LICKINS) RALSTON PURINA COMPANY, P.O. Box PL41, Belleville, IL 62222 (Receive two free boxes of Whisker Lickins) Send purchase seals from 5 Whisker Lickins cat food boxes.
Refund form required. 7/31/80

_____WHISKER   LICKINS BIC SHAVERS, P.O. Box 2159, Meriden, CT 06450 (Receive a free Bic 4 Shaver Set) Send 6 Whisker Lickins proofs of purchase seals for each set. Select mens' or ladies' shavers.
Refund form required. 12/31/80

NOTE: The addresses shown in these refund listings should not be used to request refund forms.

About the Author

MARTIN SLOANE is a graduate of Syracuse University, holds a law degree from New York University Law School and has an extensive background in sales and marketing. A veteran coupon clipper, he discovered early that keeping his coupons in a jumble in a shoe box saved him only a few dollars a week. He knew there must be a better way and started organizing, developing and expanding his skills. In 1977, wanting to tell other supermarket shoppers about all the money they could save, he founded the American Coupon Club and began publishing a monthly magazine, *The Supermarket Shopper*. He also authored *The Official 1979 American Coupon Club Couponing and Refunding Guidebook*. Since September, 1979, he has been writing a twice weekly column called "The Supermarket Shopper" for United Feature Syndicate. Mr. Sloane lives in Kings Point, New York with his wife and two children.

MONEY TALKS!
How to get it and How to keep it!

Buy them at your local bookstore or use this handy coupon:

Facts at Your Fingertips!

☐	11451	MOVIES ON TV (1978-79 Revised Ed.)	$2.95
☐	12419	THE BANTAM BOOK OF CORRECT LETTER WRITING	$2.25
☐	12850	THE COMMON SENSE BOOK OF KITTEN AND CAT CARE	$2.25
☐	13712	AMY VANDERBILT'S EVERYDAY ETIQUETTE	$2.95
☐	12993	SOULE'S DICTIONARY OF ENGLISH SYNONYMS	$2.50
☐	12713	DICTIONARY OF CLASSICAL MYTHOLOGY	$2.25
☐	13361	THE BETTER HOMES AND GARDENS HANDYMAN BOOK	$2.50
☐	13718	THE BANTAM NEW COLLEGE SPANISH & ENGLISH DICTIONARY	$2.50
☐	12370	THE GUINNESS BOOK OF WORLD RECORDS 17th Ed.	$2.50
☐	12843	IT PAYS TO INCREASE YOUR WORD POWER	$1.95
☐	13769	THE MOTHER EARTH NEWS ALMANAC	$2.95
☐	12910	THE BANTAM COLLEGE FRENCH & ENGLISH DICTIONARY	$2.25
☐	13893	THE COMMON SENSE BOOK OF PUPPY AND DOG CARE	$2.25
☐	12682	SEARCHING FOR YOUR ANCESTORS	$2.25
☐	11529	WRITING AND RESEARCHING TERM PAPERS	$1.95
☐	02810	HOW TO PICK UP GIRLS	$2.25

Ask for them at your local bookseller or use this handy coupon:

Bantam Book Catalog

Here's your up-to-the-minute listing of over 1,400 titles by your favorite authors.

This illustrated, large format catalog gives a description of each title. For your convenience, it is divided into categories in fiction and non-fiction—gothics, science fiction, westerns, mysteries, cookbooks, mysticism and occult, biographies, history, family living, health, psychology, art.

So don't delay—take advantage of this special opportunity to increase your reading pleasure.

Just send us your name and address and 50¢ (to help defray postage and handling costs).